The Way Lost.

Page 9.

THE

WAY LOST AND FOUND.

A BOOK FOR THE YOUNG,

ESPECIALLY YOUNG MEN.

BY THE
REV. JOSEPH F. TUTTLE, D.D.,
PRESIDENT OF WABASH COLLEGE.

PHILADELPHIA:
PRESBYTERIAN BOARD OF PUBLICATION,
No. 1334 CHESTNUT STREET.

WESTCOTT & THOMSON,
Stereotypers, Philada.

CONTENTS.

CHAPTER XI.

CHAPTER XII.

CHAPTER XIII.

CHAPTER XIV.

CHAPTER XV.

CHAPTER XVI.

PREFACE.

To win the young to a life of virtue and happiness by winning them to the cross is the main purpose of these pages. If it shall seem to some that undue prominence has been given to the external virtues and their contrasted vices, let it be answered that this is an important means of leading one to see precisely what he is and what he needs. As this volume is given to the press for the instruction of young people, it is with the prayer to Him who alone can give the increase, and whose alone is "the excellency of the power," that he may own the work and bless it in its mission.

Wabash College, Crawfordsville, Ind.
March 12, 1870.

THE WAY LOST AND FOUND.

CHAPTER I.

LOST THE WAY.

A YOUNG man at the West was once making his way through the forest to a farm some miles distant. The day was cloudy, and in a little time he became bewildered and lost. He could not tell which way was east, or which was north, or whether he was going toward home or away from it. The sensation is not an agreeable one, as those know who have experienced it. Suppose some skillful woodman had previously told the young man the curious fact that "*the moss is to be observed on the north side of forest trees,*" that here was a guide which the Indians and hunters will follow for miles and not be deceived. Ought not the young man in such a case to look for this guide to determine his direction by finding out which way was north? Or suppose his father had put in his hands a little pocket compass, telling him if he were ever lost in the woods to consult that honest guide which always pointed north, now that he is lost ought he not to do as he was told?

The young are just entering a world in which a great many people have "lost their way" in a sadder sense than the young man lost his in the woods.

For example, a certain strong-minded man had fallen into skeptical society. He was a man of great mechanical ingenuity and he had read many books, "but as concerning the faith he had made shipwreck." As the years passed away his skepticism increased, and yet his success in business engrossed his mind too much to allow him to see whither he was tending. At last he gave up business to enjoy his old age undisturbed by the distractions which hitherto had made up so large a part of his life. With leisure came an unwelcome visitor in the form of anxiety about the future. "What am I? Is there a state of existence beyond the grave? Is death the end of man? Whither am I going?" Such questions as these gave him trouble, and he was as much bewildered and lost as one could be in the trackless forests of Canada. He had thrown away, or at least ceased to feel confidence in, the only compass that ever yet was a safe guide to man, and now in his old age he was wandering about in a distracted way, like a lost man, not knowing what to do or whither to go.

Another man, whose faith in Christianity and in the Bible had been insidiously undermined by a companion, when the shadows of life's afternoon began to lengthen said to a friend: "I would give all I have to believe the Bible to be God's book, but I cannot." He said it sadly and not captiously, and as he spoke his friend thought of one who has lost his way and is unable to find it.

Sometimes we see a man so completely bewildered as in a sort of blind despair to cast himself into the arms of the Papal Church. The father of such an one originally was a member of a Congregational church, but left it for another communion in which his son was educated. All the influences about him apparently were of a kind to help him onward in life and usefulness. After he was ordained the writings of the "Fathers" eclipsed the Bible, and the essential truths of Christianity were covered by the unessential forms of the church. He became a churchman of the "straitest sect." The communion-*table* in his church was displaced by an *altar*. His sermons, and all the services which he conducted, were a grief to his brethren. His bishop mourned over him as he rebuked him, but it was all in vain. Secretly he consulted a priest of Rome and was admitted into that Church. He was an example of one form of losing the way.

Many years ago there was a man in one of our country churches whose deportment for years was unexceptionable, but at last he became infected with infidel notions. He passed through all the grades of skepticism, and was as restless in one as in another. He sneered and denounced and argued to keep up his courage, and did what he could to unsettle the faith of others. As old age came on his heart was not satisfied, and he adopted the flimsy and fanciful notions of Swedenborg. Every step he took from the time he began to doubt God's Word until he died seemed to say, "I have lost my way."

A young man left his home in the country for a residence in the city. By the influence of companions he gave up the Bible, forsook the church, profaned the Sabbath, visited drinking-saloons, gambling-houses and places more infamous. At last he became horribly diseased, and was brought home a frightful-looking object. Desperate at his situation, one day he put a pistol to his head and blew his brains out. To some who looked at him in his coffin and thought of his history his dead lips seemed to say, with an articulation audible at least to the heart, "I have lost my way."

We sometimes meet men who are consumed with the appetite for rum, and, as one indulgence goads them on to another, until they seem utterly reckless of the interest of themselves or others, and even hardened against the thoughts of death and perdition, we may say of them also, "They have lost their way."

In the newer regions of our country we find people who once were active members of some Christian church, but they found no churches at the West and had not force enough to establish them for themselves. The Sabbath gradually became a neglected day, the sacred time was devoted to pleasure or business, the family altar was abandoned, the Bible neglected and the great interests of religion laid aside. With no exaggeration we may say of such: "They have lost their way."

We sometimes see young men at our academies and colleges who have been trained with care and solicitude at home. With no little self-denial and expense, hard to be met in many cases, they have been sent thither to be fitted for some profession. But they were discouraged by the difficulties they met and neglected their studies. Idleness won for them undesirable companions who led them into temptation. Dissipation and mischief were carried so far, in spite of the warnings of their teachers, that at last they were sent home in disgrace or finally expelled. What better expression can we use in describing such than by saying: "They have lost their way?"

If any one who reads these pages will turn to a subsequent chapter concerning "a bad name," he will find many suggestions concerning the ways in which thousands are ruined in character and reputation, and see that to every such case we apply this description: "He has lost his way." As referring to those mistakes which the young make in the plans and doings of life, in matters pertaining to their well-being in this life and the life to come, the interests of faith and eternal salvation, the words which stand at the head of this chapter are very suggestive:

"LOST THE WAY!"

CHAPTER II.

A GUIDE-BOOK NEEDED.

HOW can a young man avoid the danger of losing the way? Or if he have lost it, how may he find it?

A stranger in Boston was endeavoring one morning to find his way to the Lowell depôt, but after walking a long distance, he inquired of a gentleman, who told him that he had lost his way, and then very courteously went with him far enough to ensure his finding the place. Suppose the stranger had desired to go to certain places in Boston, and that some friend had put in his hands a reliable map of the city. Suppose he had described the route he was to follow, and then told him, "If you lose your way, you must refer to the map." What better direction could he have given? The stranger attempts to thread his way through the irregular streets, but soon finds he has lost his way. He now opens his map, and by comparing it with the names of the streets on the street-corners, determines where he is and which way he must go to reach the place he is seeking. But what would you say of him, if, having lost his way, he should not consult his map, nor ask those who knew how to guide him, but should go heedlessly on as if by some *chance* he would find the place?

Some years ago a gentleman was about to cross a range of mountains by a route which was not very plain, nor were there people there to inform him if he should get away from the right path. A friend who was familiar with the way drew a map for him. At a certain point he would find three roads. He must take the middle one. Farther on he would come to certain "cross-roads," and he must turn to the left. And thus he put down every point at which the traveler was liable to lose his road, with explicit directions which could not be mistaken by a careful observer. In this case the gentleman had no difficulty in finding his road, because he examined his little guide-book. But suppose he had put it into his pocket, and never once examined it; ought he to have been surprised to find himself lost among the mountains?

Or suppose a ship-master is making a voyage. He is furnished with the best charts, compass, chronometer, sextant and other means of determining his position on the ocean. If he will, he can easily tell whether he is nearing sunken reefs or an island, whether he is on the right course or not. What will you say of him if he never examines his chart, never looks at his compass, or takes an observation, or measures his speed, but shakes out his sails, and lets his ship drive whither she will, expecting she shall as a matter of course reach the port whither she is bound?

In the affairs of this life, men are not usually guilty of such folly. If a traveler is to cross a range of mountains where he is liable to lose his way, he seeks the most explicit directions and tries to follow them. The accomplished ship-master would as soon fire his vessel as neglect his reckonings.

Life is often called a *journey*. Is there no guide-book containing explicit directions to those who are setting out upon it? It is called a voyage. The young are just commencing it. Many have been wrecked and lost. Is there no chart by which they may learn how to escape the dangers of this life-voyage?

CHAPTER III.

THE GUIDE-BOOK FOUND.

THERE has been no lack of guide-books for those making the momentous journey toward "the undiscovered country" whose hither boundary is the grave. Which of them is reliable? We occasionally hear of ships being wrecked on sunken reefs not mentioned in the charts. Which of these many guide-books gives all the information that we need in our journey to the eternal world? Which of these many charts maps out the course we are to pursue in order to reach the port in safety? There is but one answer: The *Bible* is that guide-book—the *Bible* is that chart.

Many people speak lightly of "the doctrines" of the Bible, as if they were lifeless skeletons wired together with a kind of dead logic. Perhaps the peculiar doctrines of one Church and another may be obnoxious to this charge, but the essential doctrines of the Bible are "life and power." The Bible teaches us the *truth* about God, about ourselves, about a Saviour and about salvation. The doctrines of repentance and faith, the work of the Holy Spirit and God's grace, are as essential to our spiritual welfare as air is to our physical life. The more we examine the doctrines of the Bible, the clearer shall be our conviction that the Bible is in truth "*the Book.*"

But the Bible teaches by *examples* as well as by doctrines. It is a book of brilliant pictures, illustrating the beauty and safety of goodness and the hatefulness and danger of wickedness. Look at our first parents in the garden. How impressive the lesson to one who is tempted to do what God has forbidden! Or look at Abraham, by the direction of God going to a strange country, "not knowing whither he went," or his obedience in going to the mount which God showed him to sacrifice his only son Isaac. Here is faith taught by facts in the life of this "father of the faithful." Or look at Moses, rescued from death by the faith of his godly parents, and while he was an honored member of the Egyptian court, being called not the servant, but "the son of Pharaoh's daughter," yet choosing to suffer affliction with the people of God. Here is an example which it is safe to commend to the young.

And thus by examination we find this book full of the examples of good men and bad men, all of which seem to say to the young—

"Enter not into the path of the wicked,

"And go not in the way of evil men.

"Avoid it, pass not by it.

"Turn from it and pass away.

"For they sleep not, except they have done mischief.

"And their sleep is taken away unless they cause some to fall. . . .

"But the path of the just is as the shining light,

"That shineth more and more unto the perfect day."

In respect to its examples, where is the book to be compared with the Bible?

It also supplies the most powerful *motives* to right action. Every page is full of motives, addressed to us as spiritual and immortal beings. How truthful and thrilling its views of this life as a "vapor," "an handbreadth" or "a flower of the field!" How weighty its declaration about the world to come, when "these shall go away into everlasting punishment, but the righteous into life eternal!" How powerfully does it describe the loss of the soul, "where the worm dieth not and the fire is not quenched!" And how sweetly does it seek to win us to Christ and heaven by telling us of the place where "the wicked cease from troubling and the weary be at rest!"

No book is so full of motives inclining us to forsake the way of sin and follow the way to holiness and heaven. Here it is, a book of over a thousand pages, each of which speaks to us in behalf of God, saying to us: "Work out your own salvation with fear and trembling, for it is God which worketh in you both to will and to do of his good pleasure." Such a book is a safe guide to follow.

But the chief characteristic of the Bible is that it tells us of JESUS, the Saviour of sinners. Look into the other guide-books and we find no Saviour. That we are sinners is very evident, and we ask, "What shall we do?" There are many answers to this great question, but not one so satisfactory as this: "Believe on the Lord Jesus Christ and thou shalt be saved." This book tells us that "the blood of Jesus Christ cleanseth us from all sins," and that "being justified by faith we have peace with God through our Lord Jesus Christ."

Besides these higher considerations, there is no book which describes the right courses and the wrong courses of life with such accuracy as the Bible. He who follows the rules laid down in this book will never lie, or steal, or swear profanely, or commit adultery, or bear false witness, or do any other act offensive to God and hurtful to himself and the community. There is no honest business, there is no right social development, there is no kind of well-being in this life, the interests of which are not promoted by the commands of this book. This is a glorious wonder, making it to be for our good to do what this book enjoins, even if our existence did not reach beyond this life. As a directory of human action, the Bible is as superior to every uninspired book, not deriving its ideas from this source, as the sun is superior to a firefly.

In all respects this book is worthy of the most careful examination, and no young person can safely neglect this plain duty: "Search the Scriptures, for in them ye think ye have eternal life, and they are they which testify of Me."

CHAPTER IV.

A GREAT FAULT.

ONE of the great faults of our day is the neglect of the Holy Scriptures. More than three hundred years ago (A. D. 1538) the English Bible, translated by Tyndale, was given to the English nation by public edict, and the annalist Strype records its reception by the people in the following memorable words:

"It was wonderful to see with what joy this book of God was received not only among the learneder sort, but generally all England over, among all the vulgar and common people, and with what greediness God's Word was read, and what resort to places where the reading of it was. Everybody that could bought the book or busily read it, or got others to read it to them, if they could not themselves. Divers more elderly people learned to read on purpose, and even little boys flocked among the rest to heai portions of the Holy Scriptures read."

And well might they be thus eager to read God's Word in English if what Cranmer said of it in his preface to the "Bible in English" in 1539 was true:

"Here may all manner of persons, men and women, young and old, learned and unlearned, rich, poor, priests, laymen, lords, ladies, officers, tenants and mean men, virgins, wives, widows, lawyers, merchants, artificers, husbandmen, and all manner of persons of whatsoever estate or condition soever they be, in THIS BOOK learn all things—what they ought to believe, what they ought to do, what they should not do, as well concerning almighty God as also concerning themselves and all others."

It is a fault of our age that the Bible is not as eagerly read as in some former generations. Undoubtedly it is in the hands of more people than ever before, and in a certain way it is studied by more people, but is not the eager search, the strong relish of former generations wanting among us? Bibles have been multiplied a thousand fold, and Christian benevolence has put "THE BOOK" within the reach of the poorest.

But the printing-press has not been idle in producing other books. How vast the increase of books of history, philosophy, science, theology, poetry and other useful and valuable kinds! Who has not felt his own insignificance and the brevity of his life as he has stood in the midst of a great library from whose shelves there looked down upon him the thousands of books which have been written by the wise and learned of past generations! One would need to live a thousand years to read all the really good books which have been written. But even these in our day are eclipsed by books and reading matter of another sort. The press is flooding the present generation with every kind of "light reading." It prints, in numbers like the leaves of autumn, the novel and the novelette, the romance in verse and prose, and every sort of book and paper to *amuse people.* Besides these, and overshadowing them, we have the *newspaper,* which penetrates myriads of dwellings, carrying thither their principal reading. In 1850 the census of the United States presented the following facts: There were 2526 different newspapers and periodicals, the number of whose subscribers was 5,183,017, among whom were circulated each year 426,409,-

978 copies! In 1860 there were 4051 newspapers, and their circulation amounted to 928,000,-000 copies! That is, in ten years the number was doubled.

It has come to pass, in this increase of light books and of newspapers, that multitudes of readers are very slightly acquainted with the really valuable books within their reach. The reason is plain. They read a book for amusement and not for mental and moral growth; they read the newspaper for the same reason that they listen to a village gossip. In this greediness for the newspaper and the book of amusement, really good books must remain very much neglected in the background. It is impossible to read a daily newspaper with any care, and a tithe of the new works of fiction even of the best class, and yet have much time for more substantial reading. This is true of men of leisure, and how much more true must it be of those who labor!

But the saddest result of these countless publications just named is not that they eclipse the masters of Greece and Rome, the grand old books in our own language, Bacon and Newton, Shakspeare and Milton, Gibbon and Hume, and such like; the rich books of a later day—Macaulay and Bancroft, and Prescott and Motley, and Irving and a hundred others. That the books of such writers should be placed in the shade is bad enough, but not so bad as that the BIBLE should be overshadowed by this pernicious literature, which, like fogs, obscures this glorious sun which God placed in the heavens to give light to the world. It is to be feared that thousands *do not read the Bible at all,* and that other thousands give it only a very superficial and hasty perusal.

The fault here described is as unjustifiable as if a mariner should have the most reliable charts and nautical instruments, and yet should either not consult them at all or do it very carelessly and infrequently. There is no other book concerning whose commandments and statutes it may truly be said, "More to be desired are they than gold, yea, than much fine gold; sweeter also than honey and the honeycomb. Moreover, by them is thy servant warned, and in keeping of them there is great reward."

CHAPTER V.

HEARING.

OUR blessed Lord repeatedly speaks to us about hearing: "He that hath ears to hear, let him *hear;*" "Take heed *what* ye hear;" "Take heed therefore *how* ye hear." Hearing implies a speaker, and therefore the exhortation has a threefold meaning—take heed *whom* ye hear, take heed *what* ye hear and take heed *how* ye hear.

WHOM TO HEAR.

Thousands are ready to take heed to what Satan says who have no ears to hear when God speaks. Eve believed not God, who said, "Ye shall not eat of it, neither shall ye touch it, lest ye die;" but she did believe Satan when he said, "Ye shall not surely die." In this very singular line of conduct many of the descendants of Eve have borne a very striking resemblance to her.

When *Jesus Christ* speaks, all should hear. From the overshadowing cloud a divine voice said of Christ, "This is my beloved Son in whom I am well pleased, *hear* ye HIM." So also spake an Apostle: "See that ye refuse not Him that speaketh; for if they escaped not who refused him that spake on earth, much more shall not we escape if we turn away from him that speaketh from heaven." If Jesus Christ is the Son of God, if he took on him our nature and suffered for our sins, then ought we to give diligent heed to him when he speaks.

But all should take heed as to *the religious teachers* they hear. A corrupt tree cannot bring forth good fruit; a religious teacher whose life is immoral cannot be a safe expounder of religious truth. This was an argument which the hypocrites could not withstand when Christ was in the world, and it was the sharp-edged sword which Luther wielded against such religious teachers as Tetzell. Any immoral man who teaches false religion in the bar-room, or workshop, or field, should be avoided as a leper whose touch is not merely pollution but death. In a small village there was such a teacher whose wit drew around him certain young men, and though he has been dead many years, they, with scarce an exception, are to this day bound hand and foot with the pernicious skepticism which he taught them.

But when a good man preaches or teaches the wholesome truths of God's word we should take heed to hear him, for he comes to us with a message from the Lord, and his words may become life and peace to us. Take heed *whom* ye hear.

WHAT TO HEAR.

But the second direction is not less important: Take heed *what ye hear*. The human soul is susceptible of deep and lasting impressions through hearing. A single remark may turn a soul toward heaven or toward hell. A very excellent minister traces his conversion to hearing a single exclamation addressed to him by a devoted Christian. The searching discourse of the evening had not moved him, but when the good man laid his hand on his shoulder and said "*O Eli!*" with emotion so deep that he could go no farther, he had winged an arrow into that hard heart.

Ordinarily, however, the results of hearing are gradual. The instructions of a pious parent are often like buried seed. Thus too the counsels of a pastor may not yield fruit at once, but the promise is that he "that goeth forth and weepeth, bearing precious seed, shall doubtless come again with rejoicing, bringing his sheaves with him." But whether the results of hearing be instantaneous or gradual matters not. Therefore let the young take heed to hear *the Bible.*

Some men, and even some very young men, discourse flippantly on the high themes of religion and immortality in our stores and bar-rooms; they denounce this doctrine and approve that; they adjudicate the claims of this book and of that to the attention of mankind, and very learnedly pronounce the Bible an imposture! A young mechanic in a certain village who has education enough barely to reckon up his small accounts, and who has never read one quarter of the book, will hold a crowd of young men listening to his denunciations of *that* Book. A great many people of diversified gifts—the learned and the ignorant, the witty and the stupid, the high and the low—have tried to smother out the light of that one Book, to make the world believe it to be a worthless book, a false book, a bad book. But they have not succeeded in their efforts; for to-day that glorious old Book smiles on the pigmies who have sought to destroy it, as surely as Mont Blanc would on the same feeble creatures should they try to uproot him from his everlasting foundations. That old Book speaks to all a message well worth their heeding. It speaks of God, oh how solemnly! How it speaks of the undying soul, destined to be for ever with the Lord or to dwell in everlasting burning! How it describes sin as odious to God, and destructive of happiness in this world and in that which is to come! How that old Book speaks of the love of God in Christ! How solemnly it speaks about hell! How sweetly does it speak about heaven! Shall we stop our ears against this Book which speaks such things with authority, and give heed to the clashing opinions and the unsustained guesses of uninspired men who reject the Bible?

"This is the judge that ends the strife
When wit and reason fail;
My guide to everlasting life
Through all this gloomy vale."

In our day the vast majority of authors write to *amuse* mankind. Thousands of public speakers have no higher aim than to tickle their hearers, who in turn have no higher wish than to be tickled. In contrast with this, the Bible is *a very earnest book.* There is not one jest or trifling word in the eleven hundred pages of the Bible. The proclamation of God's law was not made to amuse mankind, as the trembling multitudes by Mount Sinai plainly showed. Solemn as the judgment-day, the Bible sketched in fire the Law as showing what Jehovah commands us to be and to do.

"But thanks be unto God for his unspeakable gift!" If the Law is a holy Law which can only work wrath to the sinner, the Bible speaks of the "glorious gospel of the blessed God." It tells how God loved the world, and "that it is a faithful saying, and worthy of all acceptation, that Christ Jesus came into the world to save sinners." It invites the starving to the gospel feast, the thirsty to the living water, the hell-deserving to Christ. There is nothing in this gospel that is not perfectly glorious. It reveals God in Christ gloriously reconciling the world unto himself. It offers to perishing sinners a glorious salvation. It is nothing less than "the glorious gospel of the blessed God." "Take heed *what* ye hear." Bad men may amuse us with ribald jests on holy things, infidels may amuse us with awful triflings, eloquent men may discourse to us about this thing and that thing, but let us turn away from them to heed the gospel. How solemn are the words of Jesus himself! "Whosoever *heareth these sayings of mine,* and doeth them, I will liken him unto a wise man, which built his house upon a rock. And the rain descended, and the floods came, and the winds blew, and beat upon that house, and it fell not, for it was founded upon a rock. And every one that heareth these sayings of mine, and doeth them not, shall be likened unto a foolish man, which built his house upon the sand. And the rain descended, and the floods came, and the winds blew, and beat upon that house, and it fell, and great was the fall of it." Take heed that ye hear "the glorious gospel of the blessed God," which shall assuredly prove unto you either the savor of life unto life or of death unto death.

HOW TO HEAR.

If a man were very sick he ought not only to employ a physician, but give attentive heed to his advice. Hence we ought to hear religious truth as if *our lives depended on it.* Listlessness in hearing the messages of heaven is both criminal and foolish, yet how many are guilty of it! God tells us that as sinners we are sinking to hell, and yet we hear listlessly. God tells us that Jesus Christ died to save us from our sins and from hell, but we hear this truth listlessly. A listless hearer of truths awful as hell, glorious as heaven! What a strange being is man!

But we should *hear with candor*. You may look at a very beautiful landscape through a pane of red glass and the entire landscape shall look as if it were red. Prejudice imparts a false coloring to objects at which we look. It causes us to magnify the faults and to undervalue the virtues of the person against whom we entertain the feeling. Candor of spirit is to the soul what a clear, healthy eye is to the body. Religious prejudice is both odious and dangerous. It prompted the Jews to attribute the good deeds of Christ to Satan, and to construe his divine words when on trial into blasphemy. It led the Athenians to call Paul a babbler and the blessed gospel of God foolishness. In our religious concerns we risk our souls by indulging prejudice. Here we need a candid spirit. "Take heed *how* ye hear."

We should hear also *to learn the truth*. Some

hear to be amused with fine and witty sayings or with eloquence, but such an object is unworthy of one who may be lost for ever. If one were very ill, he would not thank his physician for witty sayings or eloquent disquisitions, and the physician would think his patient very foolish for expecting such things from him. A sick man wishes to know what his disease is and what is the remedy. As sinful beings we need not amusement, but truth, and we should hear to learn the truth. The truth we should apply to our own case. Some hear for others, and have an inveterate habit of applying the truth to others. What should we think of an Israelite who had been bitten of a "fiery, flying serpent," who should say to his neighbors: "This proclamation of Moses is what you need"? but as for himself he never lifts his eyes to the brazen serpent! A sinner who is under the wrath and curse of God has much more need to hear truth for himself than for others.

We often meet with persons who seem to hear attentively and candidly, but who fail to apply the truth to their own souls. It is with them a matter of intellect and not of spiritual profit. The most awful doctrines of the Bible are to them but little more than any facts recorded in profane history. They hear the most searching truths very much as David listened to Nathan's parable, seeming not to suspect that they themselves are the sinners who are described as so wicked and in such danger. It was a wise prayer of the Psalmist which we may well offer: "Search me, O God, and know my thoughts."

But finally, we should hear the truth with a *prayerful spirit.* We are depraved beings and our prejudices against the truth are very strong. In this respect we are not candidly inclined, and in addition to this we are surrounded by many perverting influences. If God do not clarify our mental vision and open our hearts to receive the truth, we shall never be savingly benefited by any truth, however affectingly or by whomsoever it may be spoken. Paul may plant and Apollos may water, but God must give the increase. Therefore, whenever we hear the truths of God's Word, our prayer should ascend to Him who giveth wisdom liberally to them that ask it, even as the Psalmist prayed: "Teach me thy way, O Lord, and lead me in a plain path, because of mine enemies."

CHAPTER VI.

HABIT.

"CAN the Ethiopian change his skin, or the leopard his spots? Then may ye also do good that are accustomed to do evil." No fuller's soap can make the Ethiopian's skin white, and though the spots of the leopard should be dyed, in due time they would reappear. The prophet compares the bad habits of his countrymen to these fixed facts. We are not to understand that a sinner is no more to be blamed for his strong habits of sin than the Ethiopian for having a black skin, but that sinful habits are very hard to change—so hard that they are not likely to be changed without the grace of God.

THE NATURE OF HABIT.

Of one person we say, "His habits are good," and of another, "He has fallen into bad habits." We speak of punctuality as "a good habit," and profane swearing as "a bad habit." The word "habit" is in constant use in the social and business intercourse of life. A parent wishes to employ a teacher for his children, or a merchant a clerk, and each inquires into "the habits" of the candidate. One principal charm in biography consists in the narration of the habits of those whose lives we are reading, and some of the most thrilling passages in history refer to the habits of such men as William the Silent, the Duke of Marlborough and Napoleon Bonaparte.

What then *is* habit? Sometimes the derivation of a word throws light on its meaning. Habit is derived from a Latin word, and means "*something had,*" that is, a possession which is not easily parted with, for instance, the Ethiopian's skin or the leopard's spots.

But the same derivative gives us another shade of meaning which is also very striking. A habit is something *worn.* A man's clothes are his habit. Blend these two notions furnished by its derivation, and they give a very forcible meaning to the word. It is a condition of body, mind or heart which is like a fixed property, of which we cannot rid ourselves even though we may wish to do so. For instance, how firm, how inveterate the drunkard's habit! How very hard it is to cast it off!

But habit is like a person's clothes. It is worn, it is visible, and it is that by which we know him. A person's habits are his outer garments, which he always wears, and which others always see. They are not the rich, showy, bridal presents which are occasionally displayed, but they are garments worn all the time. These habits are permanent fixtures, which we always wear about us and by which we are known. Thus we know one man not by his rent-rolls, but by his hard-fisted, avaricious habits. We know another not by his reputed fortune, but by his habits of generosity and kindness.

Look now at the nature of habit, in the light of the *process by which it is formed.* One has defined it to be "the effect of custom or frequent repetition." A wagon wheel running many times in the same place makes a rut. In this way ruts are worn even in very hard rocks. A stream of water flowing over the same reef of rocks will gradually wear for itself a channel. It is even so with habit. It is formed by the *repetition of similar acts.* Thus in the use of tobacco, rum and opium a habit is formed by taking the poison repeatedly.

The most delicate female may, if she choose to do so, acquire the habit of chewing or smoking tobacco or drinking rum.

Mental habits are formed in the same way. Some pupils avoid the hard parts of a lesson, and in due time this course ripens into a habit which will be very much like a mental weakness. Some persons form such a habit of reading fiction that the eloquent periods of Gibbon, the elaborate simplicity of Hume, the artless narration of Irving, and even the unapproachable pages of Bible history, have not a single charm for them. This pernicious habit has as marked peculiarities as the habit of using tobacco or opium; it destroys the memory, weakens the reason, blunts the affections, incapacitates the whole being, until in some cases the victim of fiction becomes almost or quite an idiot.

The same law prevails in moral habits. A gentleman once said of a third person, "He is so in the habit of lying that I do not think he *can* speak the truth." You sometimes hear it said of one person, "He will do just what he promised, because such is his habit," but of another person it is said, "His word is not to be relied on, for he is not in the habit of keeping his word."

In all these and many other cases the habit, whether good or bad, is formed by the repetition of acts. One dram does not make the habit of drunkenness, but it is the frequent repetition of the act which brings about the result. It is not the going to church on a single pleasant Sabbath morning which produces the habit of going to church. The gambler does not become such by one game of pitching pennies, or the purchase of one lottery-ticket, or by risking money once at the faro-bank or billiard-table, but by the repetition of such acts he begets in himself the rapacious and villainous disposition to win money which can only be won by robbery. The repetition of acts, whether good or bad, wears the channel deeper and deeper, and thus throws light on the nature of habit.

There is one singular fact which throws light on the nature of habit. When any habit becomes confirmed, it becomes *in a measure involuntary.* The Rev. Dr. Ely, of Philadelphia, once related the fact that a converted sailor, who had been very profane, in telling his religious experience used a very profane and indecent expression to show how wicked a sinner he had been! He used the oath involuntarily from the force of habit. Near the town of D——, in Ohio, lived a man and his wife who had both been profane swearers. The wife was converted, and one night, apparently in agony about her husband, she entreated him to "go forward to the altar," and when he refused, she pressed the matter, involuntarily using one of the oaths to which she had been previously accustomed! It was the force of habit, and this fact gave her a great deal of trouble and sorrow. A certain man who had been a confirmed sot for many years was converted, but to the day of his death he retained the motions and looks and ways which he had acquired when a drunkard. We see this involuntariness of a confirmed habit in the peculiar phrases which some persons use in conversation; and the same is true of some offensive habit in persons who lead the devotion of others. The habit of sleeping, or lounging, or inattention in church is a sort of involuntary habit with some, which is like a deep rut, quite hard to get out of, or, like a deeply worn channel, very difficult to change.

These illustrations are derived principally from habits which should be avoided, but the same general principle is true of those habits which should be acquired, with this difference, that in our present condition it is easier to acquire bad habits than good ones, and that at the same time it seems to be far easier to change good habits than it is to change bad ones.

Thus, in examining the nature of habit, we find it to be a fixed possession, not easily parted with and as constantly worn as our clothes. Its process of formation is by such a frequent repetition of similar acts that in time habit seems to become in a measure involuntary, and that it acts regularly and constantly. Such is its nature that it is proper to say some are temperate, others intemperate, from habit; that some are honest and others dishonest from habit; that some follow the narrow road that leads to life, and others walk the broad road that leads to destruction, from habit. As soon as we are born, we begin to form habits, and from the mother's arms to the grave every moment and hour we verify the saying, "man is a bundle of habits." In a very important sense habit is the centre and circumference, the beginning, the middle and the end of man.

THE POWER OF HABIT.

All that has been said of the nature of habit also illustrates its power, but let us look at this point specifically. The Merrimac at Lowell has been turned into an artificial canal which furnishes water-power to the great manufactories of the city. The natural channel is rocky, and, especially in high water, the current is swift. For ages have the waters flowed along that channel, wearing it deeper as the mountain freshets have poured through it to the sea. Enterprise has thrown a dam across that channel, yet the waters flow into the artificial channel by constraint; and should either the dam or the canal give away, the water would again seek its accustomed channel.

This is a striking illustration of the power of habit.

Here is the house in which lived and died a miser. He became very old, and as death drew on his sole pleasure was in handling his money. Just before he died he exclaimed, "Money is good enough, if we can only stay with it!" The mountain torrents had worn no deeper channel in the rock than the love of money had in that man's soul. When Napoleon was imprisoned at St. Helena, and when he was dying, his mind irresistibly ran upon those projects which had been the passions of his life. From boyhood until death his immense mental forces had poured along this channel, and there was no power but God's that could have compelled them to run into a new channel. So was it with the miser. From the time that he loaned out his first dollar until God said to him, "Thou fool, this night shall thy soul be required of thee!" the entire energies of his body, mind and heart had been set on the acquisition of wealth, so that death found him still swayed by the habit which had governed his life.

Illustrations are not wanting to show the power of vicious habit. When a certain member of Congress was entreated to abandon his cups, he made a reply which is in point: "Some can refrain from drinking, but they will not; I would refrain, but I cannot." How many drunkards bound hand and foot by this tremendous habit might say as one did say to his friend, "I wish to reform; I know this habit is destroying me; but there are times when it sweeps me along as a swollen river does a straw, and I am powerless to resist it!" Many years ago, in New Jersey lived a man of property, influence and respectability. He was an officer in a Christian church. One evening in the parsonage he burst into tears, as he said to his pastor, "I cannot keep from drinking, although I am disgracing my family, injuring the church and ruining myself!" And yet he repeated the sin again and again, until the pastor with choked utterance was compelled to read to a weeping assembly one Sabbath day the sentence excommunicating him from the church. He lived to be an old man, his conscience goaded him, and he was scared by the horrors of *mania-a-potu* and *delirium tremens*, but his drunken habit held him with a death-grip to the last.

Could young men stand by a certain grave and call to life its occupant that he might tell them his experience—how he tasted rum because others did so; how the repetition of the act gradually wore a channel in his nature through which his passionate appetite rushed, spurning control; how, moved by shame, by fear, by remorse and by natural affection, he strove to arrest and subdue that awful habit; how he struggled to free himself, and yet again and again that habit like a swollen mountain torrent swept out the feeble obstacles placed in its way, and how at last it bore him to the grave,—could such an one rise from the dead and tell young men his experience, they would realize the tremendous power of a vicious habit. Is not this tragedy of horrible experiences enacted in the life of thousands of drunkards? And yet will young men pursue the same dangerous process which has reduced these drunkards to their present condition?

Good habits are very powerful also. George W. Olney, a student in Lane Seminary, was remarkable for his prompt performance of every duty. When he was dying he fancied the time had come for him to be away to his Sabbath-school in the city. It required four young men to keep him on his bed. "Oh," he exclaimed so piteously, "do let me go to my Sabbath-school!" That was the last word he spoke, and it showed how strong was the habit he had formed of doing his duty promptly. It was only a few weeks after this that another lovely Christian died in the same seminary. For sixteen weeks had he been sick. His sufferings were peculiar in their nature and intensity, and by them he was wasted to a skeleton. He had an exquisite gift for music. Often he would become highly excited as his choir of trained singers uttered the melodies of Handel and Mendelssohn. When he was dying he sent for his choir and bade them sing some of his favorite harmonics. As they sung his eye lit up, his lips quivered, his frame trembled. For many years the singing of God's praises had been his daily habit, and now that he was dying he would have his soul encouraged and borne on the wings of holy song to the place where an innumerable company are singing that "new song."

When Joseph, pressed with the temptation by which many strong men have been slain, repelled it with horror, exclaiming: "How can I do this great wickedness and sin against God?" he showed how powerful the habit of virtue may become. So also when the aged apostle, borne by others into the assemblies of Christians, lifted his hands and said, "Little children, love one another," he showed the prevailing power of that habit which won for him the name of "the disciple whom Jesus loved."

Good habits are strong. They have been chart and compass to many young men leaving home to adventure on the broad sea of life. A certain boy, having lost his father, clung with strong affection to his mother. To lift her from poverty to comfort became the moving principle of his heart. He went to a neighboring city, but to every temptation which beset him, this habit of thinking of his mother's welfare presented a shield. It spur-

What Came of a Kite String.

Page 51.

red him on to his duty with such fidelity that his employer at last gave him a share in his business. His first earnings were given to his mother, and the first investment he ever made in real estate was in the purchase of a beautiful home for her. He is an example which may be safely imitated by such as are yet so happy as to have mothers still within the reach of filial kindness.

The young will appreciate these considerations at a later period more fully perhaps than now. They think of their single acts as trifling, and as having no important bearing on their future destiny. But they could hardly make a greater or more fatal mistake. A few years ago a man stood on the brink of the precipice below the Falls of Niagara. He sent up a kite into the air to which was attached a small cord. As it ascended it bore that small cord across the chasm. To this was then attached a larger cord, which was in its turn drawn across, and after this a single wire, then another and another, until of these little single wires the architect had constructed two cables of such strength as to bear up a bridge on which heavy trains of cars safely pass. And this wonderful result may be traced back to a little kite-string as its origin! It is even so in habits. Let the young beware of little things, for through them grow habits strong as iron.

The following words of self-history from the pen of Charles Lamb confirm with terrible emphasis this view of the power of habit:

"I wept, because I thought of my own condition. Of that there is no hope; the waters have gone over me. But if out of the black depth I could be heard, I would cry out to all those who have set foot on the accursed flood. Could the youth, to whom the flavor of his first wine is delusive as the opening scenes of life or the entering upon some newly-discovered Paradise, look into my desolation, and be made to understand what a dreary thing it is when a man shall feel himself going down a precipice with his eyes open and a passive will; to see his destruction and have no power to stop it, and yet to feel it all the way emanating from himself; to perceive all goodness emptied out of him, and yet not be able to forget a time when it was otherwise; to bear about the piteous spectacle of his own self-ruin; could he see my fevered eye, feverish with last night's drinking, and feverishly looking forward to this night's repetition of the folly; could he feel the body of the death out of which I cry hourly with feebler and feebler outcry to be delivered,—it were enough to make him dash the sparkling beverage to the earth in all the pride of its mantling temptation, to make him clasp his teeth,

> '—— and not undo 'em,
> To suffer not wet damnation to run through 'em.' "

RESPONSIBILITY FOR OUR HABITS.

The Bible teaches us that *we are responsible for the habits we form.* Thus, in connection with the inquiry, "Can the Ethiopian change his skin?" is this declaration, "*Therefore* will I scatter them as the stubble that passeth away by the wind of the wilderness." Abraham asked, "Shall not the Judge of all the earth do right?" but would God scatter these men like stubble by a violent wind for doing what they could not avoid doing, for having a habit of sin for which they were no more responsible than the Ethiopian is for having a dark skin? This of itself is sufficient to prove that God holds men responsible for their habits. They are not in his sight helpless machines, neither to be condemned for forming bad habits nor to be praised for forming good habits. If we take any prohibition or any promise of

God's word, we find that it hinges on this idea of moral responsibility. Thus the habit of avarice is alluded to: "Woe unto them that join house to house, that lay field to field." But why denounce a woe on the avaricious if they are not responsible for this most terrible habit of loving money? So also the woe pronounced against drunkards implies the same principle: "Woe unto them that rise up early in the morning, that they may follow strong drink; that continue until night, till wine inflame them!" Indeed, if we deny this personal responsibility for the habits we form, the commands, the threatenings, the promises and the entreaties which the Scriptures address to us might as reasonably be addressed to the uncouth images of a heathen temple. Hence that thrilling sentence, which has sometimes been quoted by lovers of pleasure, speaks thus to the young man, "Rejoice, O young man, in thy youth, and let thy heart cheer thee in the days of thy youth, and walk in the ways of thy heart, and in the sight of thine eyes; but know thou that for all these things God will bring thee into judgment."

But the same responsibility is also seen in the nature of habit as formed by the repetition of similar acts. If any bad habit were formed by a single act—for instance, if the drinking of rum once formed the habit of drunkenness—then there might be many cases which could be traced to mere indiscretion. Or, on the other hand, if one could believe that he was not a free agent in the formation of a bad habit, then he ought to feel no more sense of guilt for forming that habit than a locomotive does for running off the track by reason of a misplaced switch or a broken rail.

But our consciousness tells us that we cannot trace our bad habits either to indiscretion or the lack of natural power as free agents. Suppose that a young man has never seen a drunkard, and that he is entirely ignorant of the effects of intoxicating liquors. He knows nothing of these effects either from experience, observation, books or any other source. Should that young man find and drink a bottle of wine, and thus become intoxicated, you might charge that first act against him as an indiscretion. He has now some knowledge on the subject. He remembers that the liquor first made him cheerful, then mirthful, then boisterous and then deadly sick. When he was recovering from the effects of his debauch he felt wretched, but in due time he was restored. Suppose him, with this knowledge, to find another bottle of the same liquor, do you not see that he can no longer plead ignorance if he again drink? Once he has "looked on the wine when it was red, when it gave his color in the cup," and once it has bitten him "like a serpent," and "stung him like an adder." For *him* to drink *now* is not an indiscretion, but a sin of presumption.

If this be so, what shall we say of the young man who forms the habit of intemperance in our day, when experience, observation, books and living witnesses warn him against strong drink? That drunkard who dragged his wife into the storm when she was sick, so that in a week she was dead, that drunkard who died in unspeakable terror, shrieking, "I see the devil," that drunkard who at a certain depôt staggered under the cars and was crushed to death,—these and all other drunkards once had faces as ruddy, eyes as clear, limbs as strong, health as firm, as any young man who may read these pages. How did their faces become blistered, their eyes red, their limbs trembling, their health broken? Each one drank once, and then drank again, and thus continued to repeat the act of drinking until the habit was formed. Each time the foolish man drank, he acted against experience, observation and warning. His habit sprang from presumption and not from indiscretion.

Some young men speak of the temptations to drink which come upon them in the social circle as if they are not free to resist. These social temptations are very strong. The young especially fear the contempt of their companions, and are strongly inclined to go wherever the current moves. To row against the stream is always irksome, and this is a fair illustration of the "*inability*" of which the young sometimes complain. Look at the facts of drunkenness which are before the young men, and say whether they are dragged into the circle of temptation or whether they go there as free agents. Does the young man go because he cannot help it, or because he wishes to go? The answer is plain. But further, when he finds himself in such a place of danger, is he compelled to remain there? What would become of his inability if he learned that the smallpox prevailed there? He could then flee assuredly. Or suppose the cup is pressed on his acceptance by a beautiful woman! Here his danger is extreme, but even when tempted to drink by her, his conscience still whispers to him that he is a free agent and should bid the fair temptress away. It is a very strange fact that woman often becomes the instrument of overcoming the objections of young men to intoxicating drinks. She suffers more from the intemperance of men than the men themseves. If she be a daughter and sister, what suffering she endures in consequence of the drunkenness of a father or a brother! If she be a wife or a mother, who can tell her anguish at the drunkenness of a husband or a son? Woman suffers more acute and unendurable troubles from intemperance than from any other social evil, and it is therefore amazing that she should consent for any reason whatever to minister in the slightest degree to this custom which has cost her so much! Yet if the most beautiful and fascinating of women should "kiss the brimming wine-cup with her own lips," and pass it to the young man, a temptress hard to resist, a temptation hard to overcome, yet he hears a voice of authority saying to him, "Look not on the wine when it is red, when it giveth his color in the cup, when it moveth itself aright; at the last it biteth like a serpent, and stingeth like an adder," and his conscience says to him, "*This* is the voice of God, and you disobey it at your peril!"

It is thus with any evil habit. The single acts which repeated make the habit are freely committed by the free agent, who thus becomes responsible not only for each sinful act, but the habit to which it leads. A bad habit is not a calamity in the sense that a fire or plague or famine is a calamity. It is the result of one's own voluntary sinful acts. No one can shift the responsibility of a bad habit from off his own shoulders.

This is a truth of very great practical importance to the young. Let them now look at this truth as they will at a future day, for time may correct our theories and opinions, but not our habits. The young may put but little value on these views now, but the time will come when they may become so involved in some evil habit as to cry out in distress, "Oh that we had been wise!" The responsibility of forming any habits, whether good or bad, rests on each one, and the day will come when the young will either bless God for the grace which led them to form good habits, or reproach themselves with unsparing condemnation for the folly which led them to form evil habits. The responsibility rests on the young, the process of formation is going on, and soon the result will be reached.

READ THIS CHAPTER ON HABITS CAREFULLY.

Some one has well said, "I look at the young with profound interest because I know their dangers. Some of my early companions have already fallen victims to evil habits, whilst others of our number are walking in the high places of the earth, because God enabled them to form good habits. One who recited with me was tempted to indulge in a vice which must here be without a name. He had fine talents, he was finely educated, he had wealth and his professional prospects were very flattering, but he died the victim of his bad habits before he was thirty years old. Another of our number was the most active and skillful player at our school-games; he was a beautiful specimen of health; his social position was highly advantageous to success in life; and his friends expected great things from him. But he became habituated to drinking intoxicating liquors, by means of which he was dismissed from lucrative posts again and again. His patrimony melted away in due time. So sensible was he of the power of his evil habit that he voluntarily sought refuge in a public asylum. For a few months everything seemed encouraging, but so fearfully had his moral power been weakened by this habit of drunkenness that after a time he began to drink as madly as ever. At last in the frenzy of delirium tremens he committed suicide."

The young are likely to pursue widely different destinies. Some shall wreck themselves on the bad habits they are now forming; others attain the haven in safety. Would God they might be warned effectually to beware of any act which may lead them to a bad habit, and encouraged to such conduct as may be pleasing to God! One bright morning in May I stood in my garden admiring the goodness of the Lord as displayed in the works of his hands. I looked on our mountains, again green by this miraculous resurrection of spring. I looked on the trees covered with blossoms, filling the air with fragrance, and I exclaimed: "Oh what a beautiful world the Lord has made!" As I stood there admiring the wonders of the Lord's hand, offering my adoration to Him whose goodness permitted me again to look on the blossoms, I saw a little bird perched on the topmost bough of a tree. The breeze gently swayed the bough hither and thither, and there sat the bird pouring out a song so sweet, so joyous and so in harmony with the scene that it affected my heart, and I said to myself in Luther's words: "Oh that men would praise the Lord even as this little bird does!" The great God is in our world everywhere manifesting his goodness and power and wisdom. Why should we dwell in the midst of these glories with less gratitude than the birds? But we have God's written word, and ought to form the habit of searching it. Let not the newspaper, the work of fiction or any uninspired book supplant the Bible in our affections. Sir Walter Scott, when he was dying, said to his friend: "For a dying man there is but ONE book!" Neglect of the Bible is inconsistent with any permanent improvement. But not only should we cultivate this habit of searching the Scriptures, but practice every good habit, carefully avoiding every bad habit. Let every thought and word and action confirm us in such habits as God may approve, and let us beseech the Lord for his assistance. Remember these words: "Can the Ethiopian change his skin or the leopard his spots? Then may ye do good that are accustomed to do evil." "If thou be wise, thou shalt be wise for thyself; but if thou scornest, thou alone shalt bear it."

Reader, let me ask you to dwell upon this chapter on habit.

CHAPTER VII.

A GOOD NAME.

THERE is scarce a young man who has not looked on riches with strong desire. The elegant dwellings of the rich, their exemption from many hardships endured by the poor, the consideration accorded to them by society and the power which they have, all unite to make riches a very desirable object. But the wise man says, "A good name is rather to be chosen than great riches."

A good name includes the two ideas of a *good character* and *good reputation.* The word *character* is derived from a Greek word which primarily means an instrument used in cutting impressions on precious stones. This gradually was changed to signify the impression itself cut on the precious stone. The word conveys an idea of fixedness. The character is *what a person is* before God, and not necessarily what his associates think him to be. This last is *reputation.*

By a *good* character is not meant merely a good reputation among men, nor yet a perfectly holy character, for "there is not a just man on the earth, that liveth and sinneth not," but a character which arises from the gracious working of the Holy Ghost in the heart—a work which goes on to perfection, until at last God, working in that heart "to will and to do of his good pleasure," has prepared it for the society and enjoyments of his own immediate presence.

THREE REASONS.

A good character is rather to be chosen than great riches, and that for three reasons: First, because *God loves him who has a good character.*

God evidently regards beautiful things with delight. He has created a profusion of beautiful objects. The mountain, the landscape, the clouds, the flowers, the grain-field, the sunbeam, the snowflake, all are beautiful. Our world, notwithstanding the curse, is a very fair world, in which the Lord "hath made everything beautiful in his time." But in those things which are morally beautiful God has especial delight. He loves the humble soul so much that "thus saith the Lord, The heaven is my throne, and the earth is my footstool, . . . but to this man will I look, even to him that is poor and of a contrite spirit, and trembleth at my word." The Beatitudes spoken by our blessed Lord are an affecting proof of God's delight in a good character. "Blessed are the poor in spirit," "Blessed are they that mourn," "Blessed are the meek," "Blessed are they which do hunger and thirst after righteousness," "Blessed are the merciful," "Blessed are the pure in heart," "Blessed are the peacemakers." Such were the benedictions pronounced on those who have a good character in the sight of God. The full value of a good character in this respect cannot be known until the Judge of all the earth say to those who possess it: "Come, ye blessed of my Father, inherit the kingdom prepared for you from the foundation of the world." Then, if not sooner, it will be seen that a good character is better than great riches, because God loves such a character.

Again, a good character is better than great riches because *it is an unfailing comfort to him that possesses it.* Some possessions bring with them no comfort. David had taken Bathsheba, but his soul was afflicted with a sense of sin, which he confesses, and of blood-guiltiness, from which he prays to be delivered. Judas had the thirty pieces of silver actually in hand, but he cast them away from him with the bitter self-condemnation: "I have sinned in that I have betrayed innocent blood." Whenever bad men look at their own character they are not comforted, however they may be praised by their fellow-men. The man who has robbed widows' houses feels mean in his own eyes, even though for a pretence he may make long prayers. If one has been guilty of some great crime, the memory of it will haunt him. A certain murderer in New Jersey confessed that there had not been a moment since the fatal act when he had not been haunted with the piteous petitions of the man he was murdering. In this world very often a bad character is the source of unspeakable anguish; in the world to come it shall be like the undying worm and the unquenchable fire.

But a good character is the source of unfailing pleasure. What delight does the consciousness of having served God with a pure heart afford him who is thus blessed! He may be persecuted for righteousness' sake, and yet he is blessed. Like Paul and Silas he may be scourged as a disturber of the public peace, and be thrust into an inner prison, and there have his feet made fast in the stocks, yet can he pray and sing praises to God. His comfort is not solely, nor even principally, dependent on those outward circumstances which many regard as essential. He may be poor, sick, bereaved, despised, and yet he may be happy in the consciousness that he loves God, who first loved him. He may be so happy in this consciousness as to be able to speak of the greatest earthly trial as "this light affliction which is but for a moment."

Take such a person as Joseph, and who does not perceive that his good character must have been an unfailing source of personal pleasure? In the prison Joseph must have been refreshed with the memory of his own filial love to his father and his virtue in resisting the temptation which had resulted in his imprisonment. Who can deny that Moses also must have had a part of his reward "for choosing to suffer affliction with the people of God" in the consciousness of having done right? By the grace of God he had made a choice the thoughts of which never discomforted him. It is so with every one who has a good character. It is an unfailing source of comfort, and is therefore rather to be chosen than great riches.

There is still a *third* reason for putting so high an estimate on a good character. It is the only sound stock on which to *graft a good reputation.* Our reputation is the estimation in which we are held by our fellow-men. In certain circles the Apostle Paul had a bad reputation. Many of his "kinsmen according to the flesh" believed him to be an apostate and a bad man. In the sight of God his character was good, but his reputation was not good among his enemies. On the other hand, Hazael's character was so bad that he was ready to murder his master, and yet such was his good reputation that no one, so far as we know, suspected that he was capable of such wickedness. Some old divine quaintly traced out this distinction between character and reputation in expressing his belief that he should see some on the right hand of the Judge whom he expected to see on the left, and some on the left hand of the Judge whom he expected to see on the right! In each case the reputation of the individual would not correspond with his character.

But while such a discrepancy is not only possible, but easy, it is plain that a good character is the only sound foundation on which to build a good reputation. We sometimes see a tree which has no roots planted and putting out buds and leaves, but those buds and leaves are sure soon to wither away. Even so a good reputation which does not grow out of a good character is very likely to wither away for want of vital nourishment. A house may be built on the sand and seem to stand firm, but when the rains descend, and the winds blow, and the floods come and beat on that house, it falls because it is built on the sand. Even so a good reputation not founded on a good character may appear well until temptation and trial like angry floods beat upon it. But let the good reputation be the fair and honest index to the good character, let the man seem to others to be what he actually is, and then he will stand like a rock in the midst of the waves.

A GOOD REPUTATION.

It is said that King Pyrrhus sought to corrupt the Roman ambassador Fabricius, and that the Roman replied to him: "You shall keep, if you please, your riches to yourself, and I my poverty and my *reputation*." In his own estimation, and also in that of his adversary, his reputation for strict integrity was better than riches. With such a reputation his countrymen did not fear to trust him with any responsibility. It was so with Aristides the Just, of Athens. Themistocles was a brilliant and great man, but the people feared to trust him, whilst in Aristides they reposed unlimited confidence.

In every community there are cases which illustrate the value of a good reputation. There are men reputed to be so poor, so upright, so unselfish, that their neighbors are ready to entrust them with all they have. Their word is as good as a bond, their truth is undoubted, and in every position they may be relied on implicitly. This is indeed a very enviable excellence to attain, and it is a matter of surprise that the young seem so reckless as to what they are doing to secure either a good or bad reputation. Some seem to take pleasure in the utter destruction of a good name, forgetting how difficult it is to restore to purity a reputation which has been stained by wrong-doing.

Many years ago a boy of much more than ordinary ability pursued a course which forfeited the confidence of those who knew him. His brilliant talents were admired, but his integrity was doubted. When he was of age he removed to a distant State, and there began his career among strangers with some conduct which exhibited talent and *hypocrisy*. In the course of time, to all appearance he was converted, but many prophesied that "he would soon show the cloven foot." He became a preacher of rare merit, and his life was not merely unexceptionable, it was highly exemplary, and yet many who knew him said, "He is still acting a part." Years rolled away, and this man's talents and piety had placed him in a high position in the church of which he was one of the brightest lights, and yet after he had proved his sincerity and piety through many years, an old acquaintance said of him: "I have never been able to rid myself of the notion that he is playing the hypocrite, and I am not alone in this. We who knew him of old stand in doubt of him to this day!"

A bad reputation is not as easily exchanged for a good one as a spotted garment is exchanged for a new one.

We need to look closely at this matter of a

bad reputation in order to appreciate the value of a good reputation among men.

There was a certain man whose reputation was such that men expected to hear of his having done some base thing soon after *professing* to be converted, which he often did. He was thoroughly corrupt, so that those who knew him thought nothing too bad for him to do. They did not believe his assertions, and even his note was worthless if not secured by some responsible name. People stood in dread of him, and when he was buried many no doubt pitied his fate who did not mourn his absence. A bad reputation is a very unproductive possession, calculated to make him who has it thoroughly despised and wretched. The wealth of Solomon would be no compensation for carrying such a reputation as Ahab's or Herod's. In what striking contrast with this is the confidence which men repose in him who has a good reputation, and the admiration he excites even among bad men! Such a man may be poor, but yet he is noble. He may have very humble gifts, but his integrity is a diamond which the wealth of Crœsus cannot buy. And when he dies men exclaim: "Mark the perfect man, and behold the upright, for the end of that man is peace!"

SAMUEL PAINE.

When the Holy Spirit has sanctified the character so that the excellences of the inner man irradiate the face and unfold the character of the Christian man before others, we pay an involuntary homage to it.

Some years ago a student at the Bloomfield Academy, in New Jersey, named Samuel Paine, achieved a great reputation for piety. He was not remarkable for any other quality. His talents were not more than ordinary, and his scholastic attainments were limited, but his humility, his steady principle, his cheerful faith, his joyful assurance, were such as to win for him the confidence of all who knew him as one who walked with God. For years he had not a doubt of his acceptance with God, and this assurance of faith seemed to make his very face to shine.

A friend met Samuel Paine some years ago on an Ohio steamboat. He had been preaching in Iowa, and on his return to remove his family to that state, he embarked at St. Louis on a steamer for Cincinnati. For a day or two his modest and cheerful piety seemed to charm all who came in contact with him, but one morning, on leaving his state-room, he found that he was avoided. All his efforts to engage others in conversation were repulsed, and in some cases rudely. This was hard to bear, especially as for some time he could not learn the reason of the change. This was communicated to him at last in a very trying way. A wealthy Southern planter coming up to him cursed him as "an abolitionist," and struck him in the face. But Mr. Paine showed his piety in his evident want of disposition to resent the insult. His face was as serene after the blow as it was before, and his voice was gentle as he said to his assailant, "I trust I can forgive you this wrong, and pray God to forgive you also." Without further remark, he retired to his state-room to "pray for one who had despitefully used him and persecuted him." When he left his room an hour or two afterward, the man who had struck him was the first to meet him and to say with tears, "I did you a wrong, sir, and I ask you to forgive me!" The weak had conquered the strong. Had not this excellent man entered into rest, it would not be proper thus to speak of his beautiful character, which won for him such a reputation even among strangers that they said involuntarily, "this is one of the Lord's servants," taking "knowledge of him that had been with Jesus."

If these considerations concerning a good name are correct, then are we dealing with a most interesting reality in urging the young especially to secure a good name before God and among men. We may say to them in the strong figures employed by our Lord, pluck out a right eye, cut off a right hand or a right foot and cast them from you, do anything, suffer anything, even death, rather than speak a word or do an act which shall destroy your good name. The loss of an eye or a hand, or even of life itself, is not so great as the loss of a good name. Some great and good men have been halt or maimed or blind, and the young who read these words also can part with limbs or sight, if it be the will of God, and yet be happy in the treasure of a good character and a good reputation; but when a young man parts with his good name, where shall he go to escape the savor of his bad name? In what deep cavern shall he hide so as not only to be forgotten by others, but even by himself? Do what he will, go where he will, his bad name will follow him; he can no more flee from it than from his shadow. This is in part the penalty of sin, that the sinner who has destroyed his good name may find forgiveness with God, but his fellow-men do not forget his infamy. "A good name is rather to be chosen than great riches."

CHAPTER VIII.

HOW A GOOD CHARACTER IS TO BE GAINED.

THIS train of remark would be incomplete without some directions to aid the young in *gaining such a character* and reputation as have been described. Without such directions it would be as if a very brilliant and valuable diamond had been described, and yet the place where that precious stone could be found had not been pointed out, nor the way to reach it shown. How may the young get that good name which the wisdom of God decides to be better than great riches?

INDUSTRY.

There is a volume of sound sense in that stanza of Dr. Watts:

> "In works of labor and of skill
> I would be busy too,
> For Satan finds some mischief still
> For idle hands to do."

The late Professor Stuart of Andover was accustomed to say, in a half-serious manner, that "Original sin consists in laziness;" and a very keen observer of events in his own large parish once exhorted parents to teach their children to be industrious, because if they contracted habits of indolence in worldly business, they would show those habits in their relations to God.

Many young persons lay the foundations of their ruin in habits of indolence. A person may be indolent who is compelled to work even as the lazy ox moves under the whip. Industry is a principle which prompts a person to do his duty because it is his duty. It is not a question of ease or comfort or sensibility, but simply of duty. This habit is not easy of acquirement. It is far easier to be lazy than to be industrious, so that the young man who would become industrious must needs exert force to gain the end.

See the effect of this habit in a single illustration. A young man said to a friend in reference to a plan which was of very great importance to him: "I will call on you on Thursday about this business, as I intend to visit the circus on Wednesday." Had that young man been thoroughly controlled by this principle of industry, he would not have allowed a dangerous pleasure to crowd aside an important duty. How often can we account for the singular conduct of young persons by referring to their habits of indolence! One reads a novel in preference to a history or a book of solid worth; another goes to a party of pleasure rather than to a religious meeting; another goes to the bar-room in preference to remaining at the quiet fireside of home.

This quality is not easily over-estimated in its practical relations to success in the undertakings of this life, and also to that good name which is rather to be chosen than great riches.

The most of the young, in any community, have to labor for their living. If it be necessary to spend eight, ten or twelve hours a day on the farm, at the lathe or bench or anvil, so much the more urgent is the reason why a young man should not waste his hours in the evening by lounging and dissipation in the streets, stores, saloons or bar-rooms. Yet how many young men plead the hard labors of the day as the reason why at night they should be indulged in a lazy habit which is likely to injure them seriously both for time and eternity! There are but few young men who cannot, if they be industrious, obtain an extensive acquaintance with the Scriptures which are able to make them wise unto salvation, and also the standard histories of nations and men. Young men certainly have very little prospect of getting that valuable diamond, "a good name," until they govern themselves in their pursuits and in the disposition of their time by the principle of industry, which both seeks for and does that which is right. Industry may be confidently named as an important link in the causes which result in the soul's salvation.

MENTAL TRAINING.

Another direction closely connected with the last is that, to gain a good name, it is of great importance to the young to educate their minds as far as their circumstances permit.

Some may say that such a rule can more fitly be addressed to scholars than to those who would learn how to get a good character; but it is easy to show that mental discipline is a valuable auxiliary in all right moral training. What is sometimes called a "liberal education" is not now referred to. Some pass through a course of study with very little mental profit. Their stock of knowledge may be increased, and yet their mental powers be no stronger nor more disciplined than when they began. Mental discipline is the training of the mind to obey instead of acting according to passionate impulses. For instance, there is a humble woman who has so trained her mind that she finds no difficulty in turning from her work to the word of God to commit some of its teachings to memory for the purpose of meditation; there is a mechanic whose advantages were limited who has disciplined his mind admirably by investigating the truths of the Bible and books of acknowledged merit.

The want of this mental training is a very serious obstacle in the way of the young. How many of them dread the Sabbath as a long tedious day, instead of blessing God for a whole day to devote to the consideration of the most ennobling and thrilling themes that can occupy the human mind! How many of the young falter in the attempt to fix their minds on a given subject—so much so that a chapter in the Bible or a discourse, however interesting, utterly fails to instruct them! Their minds glance off from one object to another without resting enough in one place to gain any good. In consequence of this habit their progress in the acquirement of truth is very slow, and for want of clear ideas of duty they are constantly liable to fall into the power of temptation. "Clouds are they without water, carried about of winds." To speak to such thoughtless and unreflecting persons about so interesting a theme even as a "good name" is to speak in the ear of the wind.

But when by diligence the mind of a young person is so trained that it can grasp and hold the truth, there is reason to hope that the truth will find a lodgment, and that the devil will not be able to steal it away.

BAD COMPANY.

To get a good name the young *should carefully avoid bad company.* He who associates with the bad is himself reputed to be bad, and in time usually becomes bad. "Evil communications corrupt good manners." "Can a man take fire into his bosom and his clothes not be burned?" Associations with the profane, the dishonest, the infidel, the profligate, or with those who are in any way vicious, will sooner or later make sad impressions on the character. It is far easier to assimilate the good to the bad than the bad to the good. A stream of dirty water will discolor a spring brook sooner than the spring brook will cleanse a stream of dirty water. Bad associates tear away the foundations of character which are not bedded on the eternal rock of God's word and Spirit, even as the floods sweep the foundations from under the house that is built upon the sand. There is little hope that a young person will obtain that the price of which is indeed above rubies, better than great riches—a good character before God—if he do not shun the vicious as he would the pestilence.

A certain lad seemed to be virtuous and honest in every respect. His employer trusted him implicitly, and at one time would have recommended him in the highest terms for any place of trust he was capable of filling. At length he became associated with young men who frequented the bar-room and the theatre. For a time he struggled to counteract the influence on himself, but in vain. His reputation for honesty and virtue was soon gone. Nor was this the worst of it. His character became vicious, like that of his associates, and to-day he is a poor wreck both as to character and reputation.

Another young man twenty-five years ago had as bright prospects as the most ardent could desire. He had talents of a peculiar order which fitted him to occupy a certain office of great responsibility, honor and profit. He eagerly desired and seemed sure to reach it. Hitherto his associates had been such that he would not have been ashamed to introduce them to his mother and sisters. His place in the church was occupied regularly, and in all respects as to business capacity and reputation he was excelled by but few. A change was soon perceptible in his demeanor. Occasionally he was not at church, and at times he was seen at fashionable saloons. His new associates were vicious, and in a very short time he himself became thoroughly corrupt. His employer withdrew from him the trust reposed in him, and in a few years he sank down to the lowest infamy. His reputation and character both perished before the influence of wicked associates.

Let the young remember that the vicious or infidel associate is incompatible with the gaining of a good name. The most attractive view of the excellence and the rewards of virtue and piety, the most revolting description of the hatefulness and punishment of vice and impiety, may become entirely powerless through the influence of bad associates. Alas for the young man who is thus corrupted by evil communication! He shall not have that "good name" which the Son of God shall mention without shame in the presence of his Father and of the holy angels. "Blessed is the man that walketh not in the counsel of the ungodly, nor standeth in the way of sinners, nor sitteth in the seat of the scornful!"

LUTHER'S FRUIT TREE.

They who desire to get a "good name" must study the holy Scriptures constantly, earnestly and candidly. This is a great rule, and one well worthy of repetition. That part of the Bible which had then been revealed the Psalmist calls a lamp and a light. He compares it to honey which is sweet to the taste, and to pure gold well refined. It is a marvelous book, a miracle more amazing to the thoughtful mind than the raising of Lazarus from the grave. Its history of man, the law which it proclaims and the gospel it reveals, its promises and its threatenings, its rules of life, its sublime descriptions of the future blessedness of the holy and misery of the unholy—all compose a book which has no peer on earth. It is a book which warrants the glowing eulogium of the Psalmist: "The law of thy mouth is better unto me than thousands of gold and silver." "How sweet are thy words unto my taste! yea, sweeter than honey to my mouth. *Through thy precepts I get understanding, therefore I hate every false way.*"

The word of God is to man's spiritual nature what bread is to his body. It is so essential to his well-being that it cannot be dispensed with, it matters not what substitute is provided, without serious damage. There is a nourishment in that Book which is precisely adapted to man's wants in every relation—as a child, a parent, a husband, a brother, a citizen or an heir of immortality. Take away God's word from a church or a nation, and the effect is as perceptible as if you withheld food from the body. Those men in all ages who have exhibited the Christian manhood in its most perfect fullness have loved the word of God with such a relish as the hungry have for bread. There is no substitute for this Book. It speaks with authority. Its lessons are weighty. It seems to bring God and eternity very near to him who reads it earnestly, often and candidly.

"Happy is the man that findeth wisdom, and the man that getteth understanding. . . . .

She is more precious than rubies; and all the things thou canst desire are not to be compared unto her. . . . . She is a tree of life to them that lay hold upon her, and happy is every one that retaineth her." Happy the youth who thus receives the instruction and the law of his Father in heaven, "for they shall be life unto his soul and grace to his neck."

In this age of books let the young allow no books to displace the Bible. Luther compared it to *a tree full of fruit.* As he picked and ate the fruit from one bough and then from another until he reached the topmost bough, he supposed it all to be gone, but when he came back to the limb at which he commenced, it was still full of delicious fruit. He went over that tree five times a year, and yet the fruit was never exhausted.

If the young would gain a good name, let them reverence the word of God, searching it in an earnest and candid spirit, and be sure this word of the Lord will be verified, "Them that honor me will I honor, and they that despise me shall be lightly esteemed." "Wherewithal shall a young man cleanse his way? By taking heed thereto according to thy word."

THE SPIRIT OF A LITTLE CHILD.

Another rule to guide the young in their efforts to gain a good name is to obey the commands of God with the spirit of little children. "And Jesus called a little child unto him and set him in the midst of them, and said, Except ye be converted and become as little children, ye shall not enter the kingdom of heaven." Some great orators have studied diligently parts of the Bible as furnishing a model of eloquence. Some very learned scholars, following the guidance of pride, have studied the Bible to gain the fame of scholars. Many persons read parts of the Bible as they read any other book, for the purpose of being amused. A child at home does not listen to his father's promises, threatenings or directions in this spirit. He hears in order to obey. If he is away from home and receives letters of advice or instruction from his father, he reads them that he may do what his father wishes.

This is the spirit in which the young must read the word and learn the will of God. They are not to read the Psalms because they are beautiful, nor the book of Job because it is eloquent, nor the history of Moses and Joseph because it is pathetic, nor the life of the Son of God in the gospels because it is unspeakably marvelous, nor the mighty arguments of the Apostle Paul, because they display the power of a most gifted intellect. Thus to read the word of God would be as if Saul of Tarsus had admired that bright light at noonday and the display of divine power without saying with a humble and teachable spirit, "Lord, what wilt thou have me to do?" The spirit of cheerful obedience will work wonders in casting up a highway over the valleys and in digging down the mountains. That is a delightful and comforting word of our God, when he says, "The Lord is nigh unto them that are of a broken heart, and saveth such as be of a contrite spirit."

PRAYER FOR HELP.

Finally, those who desire a good name *should pray constantly* and fervently to God for the divine assistance.

The simple facts concerning prayer may be stated in the language of the Scriptures. We are sinful creatures, hence we are taught to pray, "Forgive us our debts as we forgive our debtors." We are ignorant creatures, hence we are assured

"If any of you lack wisdom, let him ask of God, that giveth to all men liberally and upbraideth not, and it shall be given him." We are dependent creatures, hence we are told to pray, "Give us this day our daily bread." We fall very easily into sin, hence each may pray as the Psalmist did: "Hold up my goings in thy paths, that my footsteps slip not," "Hold thou me up and I shall be safe." We are liable to very grievous afflictions, hence we may imitate the afflicted Psalmist when he cried out, "Make haste to help me, O Lord my salvation." Directly and by example the Holy Scriptures teach us as dependent creatures in every relation of life to offer fervent prayer to God for divine assistance.

Nor is this a mere arbitrary statute of Heaven. Mankind acknowledge their need of help, and in their extremity call on God. The experienced and the good feel this want, insomuch that prayer and piety coexist of necessity in the same character. It is impossible to find real prayer without piety or real piety without prayer. But if the aged saint, rich in the experiences of this life, needs to pray, how much more the inexperienced youth who has just launched his vessel on a dangerous and stormy sea! There are many shoals and many false lights to decoy the young mariner, and there are many storms to threaten him with destruction. And how shall he attempt a voyage across such a sea without beseeching God to keep him safe in the hollow of his hand? The Psalmist, in his sublime description of the sailors when their vessel is pressed with the storm, has spoken a word which every youth should imitate:

"Then they cry unto the Lord in their trouble,
"And he bringeth them out of their distresses;
"He maketh the storm a calm,
"So that the waves thereof are still.
"Then are they glad because they be quiet,
"So he bringeth them unto their desired haven."

Oh how often has the weary and dependent and tempted soul cried unto the Lord in the hour of danger, and found by blessed experience that it is not a vain thing to wait on the Lord!

It is a strange fact that the young dread to be even suspected of praying. Yes, ashamed to ask help of the great God! But while this is so, it is also true that he who restrains prayer, either because of the pride of his heart or his fear of man, will not win a good character. The words of prayer are not a sign of unmanliness in a young man or in any man. Never did words so become a young man's lips as when Solomon prayed the Lord to give him an "understanding heart, that he might discern between the good and the bad." It is a great experiment we are now making, a great probation we are now spending, a great result we are soon to reach—nothing less than eternal felicity or eternal sorrow. We have a sinful heart to tempt us, and we are assaulted with temptations at every step in the way, and we assuredly shall perish if we do not ask God for assistance. We cannot without fervent and constant prayer win that good name which our blessed Saviour shall mention with approval before his Father and before the holy angels.

A MODEL JOSEPH.

This discussion of a good name would be incomplete without taking from the Holy Scriptures at least one model character as an illustration. Were the question asked, "Who shall he be?" the unanimous answer would be, "JOSEPH."

AS A SON.

In the fine arts a model is that which is to be imitated. Joseph is such a model for every young person who would have a good name. His name shines upon us as beautifully and purely as a star in the unclouded sky. His father's love for him was founded on his moral excellences, and not on mere caprice. "Jacob loved Joseph more than all his children" not because he was the youngest, for Benjamin was younger, nor because his gifts were superior to those of his brethren, for in this respect Judah's gifts were pre-eminent. The reason for Jacob's love of Joseph was this, "because he was the son of his old age." This expression is understood by many as meaning that Joseph was born when his father was an old man, but its probable meaning is that he was a son who tenderly loved and cherished his aged father. What a beautiful characteristic!

To the end of his life his love to his father never grew dim. How affecting the words he spake to his brethren after he became governor of Egypt, "Is your father well, the old man of whom ye spake? Is he yet alive?" And when he had made himself known to his brethren, he said to them, "Haste ye, and go up to *my* FATHER and say unto *him*, Thus saith *thy son Joseph*, God hath made me lord of all Egypt. Come down unto me; tarry not." When they met after so long a separation, Joseph fell on his father's neck and "wept on his neck a good while." And when Jacob died, "Joseph fell upon his father's face and wept upon him and kissed him." From his childhood until the death of his father he was a good son, and he has been a model of filial affection to this day.

AS A BROTHER.

Scarcely less admirable was his character as a brother. Never did one have more selfish brothers, and yet from first to last he treated them with a noble and disinterested affection. He told them his dreams, never thinking to excite their envy, and when they were selling him into bondage, he *besought* them, but did not *curse* them. When he met them in Egypt his heart yearned over them, and he made every preparation for their comfort. The great wrongs they had done him he forgave in a spirit that showed the goodness of his heart.

IN TEMPTATION.

Under the teachings of divine Providence the young servant was sold to Potiphar, "an officer of Pharaoh and captain of the guard." "And Joseph was a goodly person and well favored." "And the Lord was with Joseph, and he was a prosperous man; and his master saw that the Lord was with him, and that the Lord made all that he did to prosper." His master placed entire confidence in him, and under the divinely blessed labors of Joseph, Potiphar's affairs were greatly prospered. And he left all that he had in Joseph's hand, and knew not aught he had, save the bread which he did eat.

This was a most serious temptation, and had he been dishonest it would not have been a matter of surprise, since in every age young men have yielded to far weaker temptations. But Joseph resisted this temptation, and maintained his character for honesty. In this he is a noble model for the young.

But he was met by another temptation, which is described at length in the Scriptures, and to this he presented this shield, which warded off the fiery dart: "But he refused, and said unto his master's wife, Behold my master wotteth not what is with me in the house, and he hath committed all that he hath to my hand; there is none greater in this house than I; neither hath he kept back anything from me but thee, because thou art his wife: *how then can I do this great wickedness and sin against God?*"

No mere man ever uttered a nobler sentence in the midst of temptation. What shame and sorrow would it have saved millions if they had "resisted the devil" as Joseph did, saying, "How then can I do this great wickedness and sin against God?" In this respect the model is worthy of imitation.

AS A PIOUS MAN.

As the root sustains the branches, so did Joseph's piety toward God sustain all those admirable qualities which made up his good name. It was no idle boast when he said to his brethren, "I fear God." His history shows him to have been animated by true piety. When he made himself known to his brethren, he did not reproach them, but said, "Be not grieved nor angry with yourselves that ye sold me hither: for God did send me before you to preserve life." When the false witness borne by his mistress caused his imprisonment, while conducting the affairs of the prison and interpreting the dreams of the butler and baker, the same piety was visible. Not less illustrious did his faith appear as he stood before Pharaoh, as he administered the affairs of Egypt and as he was dying.

Among all mere men there is no safer model for the young to imitate than Joseph. He was a model son, a model brother, a model man. He appears worthy of imitation in the family, in temptations, in adversity and in prosperity.

CHAPTER IX.

A BAD NAME.

MIRABEAU, the great French orator and revolutionist, was exceedingly vile in his habits; his excessive indulgence destroyed him in the prime of life. While he was dying, he put his arms around the neck of his friend Dumont and exclaimed in pathetic accents, "I would pass through a furnace heated seven times to purify the name of Mirabeau! But for this name, so polluted, all France would be at my feet!" The value of a good name stands out in contrast with the loss of a bad name.

There are two phases of a "bad name," the bad *character* and the bad *reputation*.

A BAD CHARACTER.

Character, as previously stated, is a word which describes a person's real condition as a moral being. The foundation of a *bad* character is that depravity which is in every human being. "The carnal mind is enmity against God, for it is not subject to the law of God, neither indeed can be." "The heart is deceitful above all things and desperately wicked; who can know it?"

On this universal fact is based the call to "all men everywhere to repent," and the declaration of Jesus, "Except a man be born again he cannot see the kingdom of God," and "A corrupt tree bringeth forth evil fruit." As there is no exception to the depravity among mankind, so, in order to salvation, there can be no exception to this necessity of a change of heart. "Ye must be born again." Judged by this rule, there never was a perfect mere man—not one who could properly say to a fellow-sinner, "Stand by thyself; come not near to me, for I am holier than thou."

For this reason, whenever a person realizes his own depravity and sin, he does not say with the Pharisee, "God, I thank thee that I am not as other men," but with the publican, "God be merciful unto me a sinner."

From the general statement just made let us pass to one more specific and limited. Reference is made to the *presence of some vice in the heart and habits of an individual whether that fact is*

known to others or not. Judas Iscariot was *reputed* to be a good man before he betrayed Christ, but could his companions have looked into his heart they would have found it controlled by the "love of money," and that he was as truly "a devil" before his treason as he was after it.

Look at that man who stands so prominently before the world as a good man and an able minister of the New Testament. How nobly does he speak for Jesus in "the great congregation!" and how many of the Lord's saints hang on his lips as he "holds forth the word of life!" What an enviable reputation he has among men!

But follow him into one of the gilded retreats of sin; see him inflamed with passion and plunging into the whirlpool of sinful indulgence. It is a sight over which angels might weep. Look at him there, and you see that vice has wound her chains about him. As you see him there, you see his real character, and you pronounce it "a bad character" in a deeper sense than that in which it is applied to the whole human family.

Look at another. He is a husband and father, and is very exemplary in these relations. He is a religious professor, and is very efficient in the Sabbath-school. People call him a good man, and his reputation is honorable in all respects. But get behind the scenes, and see him administering poison to one who had trusted him; see him stealthily but firmly carrying forward his diabolical designs until he is guilty of murder; see him stand and weep beside the grave in which his victim is buried. There you see his real character in all its corruption. He is reputed to be a good man, but he is in reality a very bad man.

Look at another. He too professes to be, and he is reputed to be, a good man. Not unfrequently is his voice heard in prayer, and the language appropriate to communion with God seems to be natural and comely as uttered by him. When the wants of the heathen, or the feebleness of our young churches at the West, or the struggle of our young men preparing to preach, are presented, how gracefully and heartily does he respond to these claims, as if it were a favor conferred on himself personally to be allowed to contribute to such charities! How noble he appears as on a Sunday morning he overtakes some aged woman making her way to the sanctuary and lends his strength to her faltering steps! And how intelligently and sympathetically does he talk about the fundamental truths of religion! But go after him into that upper room where he supposes himself unwatched, and you see that at heart he is corrupt. Gaming and drunkenness are actual vices in his character. When you get at that character as it appears to God, it is in very deed a bad character.

Not many years ago there lived in one of our Western States a man who appeared to be a gentleman. He was the owner of a magnificent farm, in the midst of which was a beautiful mansion. Although not a professor of religion, he was constant in his attendance at church and very liberal in his contributions. He was also a man of public spirit, and in most respects a pattern held up for imitation in the community. Whilst he was carrying such fair appearances the country was flooded with the most dangerous counterfeits, so well executed as in some cases to deceive bankers of experience. Vast damage was done to business. Individuals were in many cases large losers, and many banks were straitened by the panic which was thus created, and which forced their bills back on them. The most active exertions were made to find the source of the mischief, but for a long time all efforts were baffled; no one suspected the artful and accomplished villain until one of his accomplices, whc was in jail, pointed out the man already described as the leader of a numerous gang whose operations extended to every part of the country. When this statement was first made it was regarded as a hoax, but the informant told too many facts to permit the affair to go by without investigation. Accordingly, one night a company of men quietly surrounded the man's house, and in spite of his indignant protestations arrested him and searched his premises, finding abundant proofs of his real occupation and character.

Thus we might illustrate every vice which corrupts the heart and converts general depravity into special wickedness in the form of a bad character. Here is a woman of very genial manners and great apparent truthfulness. She seems to those not intimately acquainted with her to be a most gentle, benevolent and well-disposed person, and yet she will insinuate and hint falsehoods without number and in the most heartless manner, until those who know her have ceased to believe anything she may say.

Whatever the vice may be—whether it be secret or open, whether it be dishonesty, licentiousness, falsehood, drunkenness, avarice, jealousy, maliciousness or any other vice, it gives its possessor a bad character. Irrespective of his reputation among his fellows, he is a bad man at heart.

A BAD REPUTATION.

After what has been said of a bad character it may seem needless to say anything further about a bad reputation, but the matter is too important to be passed by without distinct mention. A man's reputation defines what others think him to be. Thus one has the reputation of being an honest man; another has the reputation of being a great rogue; one has the reputation of being a Christian believer, while another has the reputation of being an infidel. This reputation may be deserved, because it accords with the actual character of the one who has it, or it may differ entirely from that character. Thus a good man may be reputed to be a bad man. For instance, a man whose moral character stood the test of death was imprisoned for a crime of which he protested his innocence, and he died with that ignominy on his reputation. He had thus a bad reputation, which was not rectified until some years after his death, when a man on the scaffold confessed that he had done the deed for which the other suffered.

As already shown, a bad man may so conduct himself as for a time to deceive others. He has a bad character, but a good reputation.

A bad reputation is the special thing now to be illustrated. Many years ago a young gentleman who had recently been graduated at one of our colleges was on his way southward in search of a situation as a teacher. His talents and attainments were more than respectable. His manners were very pleasing, and he was the owner of a good reputation at home. He had the very best recommendations with which to invite the confidence of strangers. On the same boat with him was a wealthy planter who was on the lookout for an educated teacher for his sons. He was ready to pay liberally for the services of a suitable man. The very first day they were on the boat together the planter learned the object of the young man in going to the South, and he was so favorably impressed with his manners and gifts that he resolved to make him a liberal offer provided he should see nothing to shake his confidence in him. One day the young man seated himself for a game of cards, and soon proved himself no mean adversary in the game. The planter looked at the transaction with regret, as destroying the young man's good reputation by bringing to light his real character. Before the voyage was finished the student learned that the planter was looking for a teacher, and offered his services, but was told that "his skill at cards was too suggestive of danger to one's sons to allow him for a moment to think of exposing them to such a teacher!" His bad reputation in that case had defeated his plans.

Such a reputation may apply to any vice that can be named. The one who steals, or lies, or kills, or slanders, or hates, or envies, or does any other bad deed, has a bad reputation among men. Absalom conspiring against his father, Saul seeking to assassinate David, and Joab basely stabbing Abner and Amasa, Herodias gnashing her teeth on John the Baptist, and Salome immodestly dancing before Herod and ferociously asking the head of John in a charger, acquired bad reputations. Their reputation grows no better, and never will as long as the world stands.

A bad reputation is a terrible possession for one to have.

A BAD REPUTATION AS A DAMAGE.

The evil gratifications by which a bad reputation is gained usually are momentary and trifling.

Take a case somewhat singular. One of the noblest laymen in this country once related this fact. He knew a boy who on a certain "training-day" had a sixpence to spend. Seeing a man with "peanuts and candies," he bought of him "two cents' worth." He gave the candy-man his sixpence, and received four cents in return. He had not gone far before, in examining his change, he found the man had given him a shilling by mistake, concealed between two pennies. The first thought was great delight at this unexpected accession to his wealth. The next thought was this, "It is not mine." "But it is mine," he argued with himself, "for the man gave it to me." "He did it by mistake, did he not?" said conscience. "I am not bound to look after his mistakes," he argued with himself. "Perhaps not," said conscience, "but I advise you to run to the man and give him back his money! You will lose nothing by such a course!"

At first he resolved to go back, and then he concluded to wait until he met the man. Thus a considerable time passed before he began to look, and then he could not find him. He was now feeling so conscience-stricken that he was very anxious to find him, but his searchings and inquiries were vain. He never found the man. He has been heard to say when he became rich that he would give ten thousand dollars to get rid of the self-contempt with which he was haunted whenever he thought of that incident. His gratification was short-lived, and it left him a pang which he never ceased to feel down to old age. A life of beautiful piety and benevolence could not dig a grave deep enough to bury that "dirty shilling" in.

Many mean deeds of this kind are kept secret, and yet the pleasure derived from them affords no compensation for the penalty inflicted by memory and conscience.

But the most of the evil deeds which flow from a bad character and procure for the evil-doer a bad reputation cannot be concealed. In spite of human depravity there is a sentiment adverse to the grosser crimes which sets people to watching one another, so that concealment is very difficult. Suppose a man to become addicted to drinking intoxicating liquors; some one must sell the liquors to him, and therefore the main fact is known. But not only is this true, but his drinking will be apparent in his face and his habits. He cannot be a drunkard secretly, nor can he be a gambler secretly, because he must play with some one, and in some way the fact gets out. Many men indulge in these disreputable habits, not suspecting that their conduct is known, but the old saying is verified in them: "Be sure your sin will find you out."

One fact is very singular, that transgressors have so little sympathy with one another. When Judas in his agony said to them who induced him to betray Jesus, "I have sinned in that I have betrayed innocent blood," with the most utter heartlessness they replied, "What is that to us? See thou to that." If several persons are suspected of a crime, the probability is that each one will try to shift the burden from himself to some other one.

In a retired country place was an innkeeper who sold rum in a quiet way, not wishing to be involved in the disagreeable consequences of a more public traffic. One man often visited his bar until he was regarded as a hopeless drunkard, but to the surprise of his neighbors this man reformed, and for a time appeared well. After some months his appetite for liquor revived, and he went into that tavern secretly. The landlord did not warn him to avoid the temptation, but asked him to drink! No one was present at the interview. By and by the reformed man was worse than ever. People asked how it came to pass, but the fact was not known until the man himself with bitter maledictions on his tempter stated the fact.

And thus, through the agency of conscience, the watchfulness of society, and the heartlessness of companions in sin, there are nine chances out of ten that the deeds which make a bad reputation for their doer will become public. If a young man tipple, or gamble, or pilfer, or attend improper places of amusement, or associate with immoral companions, the fact will come out, and the influence of it be felt in his reputation.

A bad reputation will be a great damage to its unfortunate owner.

THE PERMANENCE OF A BAD REPUTATION.

It is far easier to spoil a good name than to retrieve it when it is exchanged for a bad name, and in this fact we find a most emphatic warning to beware of trifling with our good name. We sometimes hear such a comment as this on the reported misconduct of some person, "I am prepared to believe it, for it is just like him!" His reputation is bad, and it is permanent.

In a certain school many years ago there was a young man who had been to sea, and among other things had learned how to tattoo the human flesh with India ink. He had not been in the school long before he had put his marks on many of his companions. He had printed anchors and serpents and ships on their arms, stars between their thumb and finger, and rings on the finger. The boys thought it very fine indeed, and often paraded the curious figures on their arms and hands, but after a while they began to wish the figures were not there, and, in fact, in their folly often resorted to soap and water in hopes to remove the stain. These stains did not yield to soap nor to any other means. What the young sailor did in a few minutes will stick to these young men through life. A bad reputation is almost as hard to get rid of as this tattooing on the boys' arms.

A good name, like a beautiful face, when once marred by misconduct, cannot be restored easily to its former beauty. Suppose a comely young man should perversely resolve to tattoo his face with hideous figures. A few hours would suffice to accomplish the folly, but no ingenuity or pains-taking would be able to remove the deformity and restore the lost beauty. A beautiful child in one moment may become hopelessly scarred by scalding, burning or an unfortunate slash with a knife. It is so with a good name. It is exceedingly hard to convert a bad name into a good name. The bad possession is easily obtained, but extremely hard to be rid of. Like a shadow, it follows and haunts its victim wherever he goes.

A young man of excellent talents and blameless reputation was attending school. His means were quite limited, and one day he found a ten-dollar bill. Instead of advertising it, he said nothing about the matter. The same day an advertisement in the "Bulletin" announced that Mr. —— had lost a ten-dollar bill. The way of restoration was open. The student, balanced on a pivot, at last determined to retain the money for the flimsy reason that its real owner was rich and would not miss it, while it was a great prize to a poor young man! Meanwhile, a description of the bill had been sent to the stores in the village, and in about three weeks the deluded finder, presenting it at a store on the opposite side of the river, was detected. He was sent away from the institution in disgrace. Afterward he was permitted to return, but his bad reputation came with him, and finally drove him away. Should he ever return to that place, he will find that the bad reputation achieved by that single act is still alive. He has removed many hundred miles from the scene of his disgrace, but a bad reputation has wings and has followed him. He will feel the influence of that mean deed until he is removed by death.

A bad reputation is like the poisoned shirt which Nessus gave to the wife of Hercules, pretending that if her husband wore it, it would keep his love faithful to her; but when Hercules put it on he could not put it off, and so the deadly gift destroyed him.

Alas for him who has so permanent a possession as a bad reputation, which he can neither sell nor give away, run from nor bury!

ONE PECULIARITY OF A BAD REPUTATION.

People are either unable or unwilling to forget the evil deeds of others.

"The evil that men do lives after them;
The good is oft interred with their bones."

Some seem to regard it as a perverseness of human nature that the wicked and mean actions of men are so carefully remembered, but the fact is not so much a proof of human perverseness as of divine retribution.

Many years ago a man named Brakeman was traveling in company with a peddler from Montrose, Pennsylvania, to Philadelphia. They crossed the Delaware at Milford, and passed through Sussex county, New Jersey. From Sparta to Woodport in that county the road crosses a mountain, and is very lonely. Not a mile from Sparta are the remains of an old lime-kiln, and very often you hear people say as they pass by it, "That was the place where Brakeman tried to push the peddler into the lime-kiln!" A mile farther east you come to a lonely place, and probably there is not a day in the year when travelers passing that way do not point out the spot where the peddler's body, "shockingly mangled, ... and the large knife and club which Brakeman carried," were found. Afterward a little tavern was built by the roadside and called "Brakeman's tavern," and subsequently the toll-gate was put up there and called "Brakeman's Gate." You go to the county seat, and the people point you to the spot where Brakeman was hung. That bloody deed will never be washed out of the popular memory, and the name of this bad man will be mentioned with horror in all time to come.

As you pass down South street in Morristown, New Jersey, you often hear persons say, pointing to a certain house, "There La Blanc murdered the Sayre family!" No doubt a hundred people every day think of La Blanc as they pass the house. His bad reputation will live for a long time to come, because the people cannot, if they would, forget him.

When Solomon said, "The name of the wicked shall rot," he did not mean chiefly that their name should be forgotten, but that it should be regarded with loathing.

What is true of such atrocious deeds is true to some extent of all wicked deeds. It seems as if a bad reputation was endowed with a sort of retributive immortality. In a certain community there lived an exceedingly interesting Christian gentleman. By many he was esteemed a model man, and in most respects he was such; but a stranger once, in making some official inquiries, stumbled on one of the "sins of his youth." Astonished, the stranger asked if this thing was commonly known. "Oh, to be sure it is! such things are never forgotten!" was the significant reply. Quite similar was another experience. A clergyman once spoke in terms of eulogy of a certain man whose funeral he was attending. Not long after a plain man asked him if he had ever heard that the deceased so many years ago did such and such mean deeds, and that in consequence people called him by a certain reproachful name. All this was new to the minister, but fresh in the popular memory.

This is a peculiarity of a bad reputation, that it survives all attempts to extinguish it. A man may seek to eclipse it by a reputation for learning, or wit, or wealth, or to hide it by unnumbered deeds of real goodness, and yet the bad reputation will survive.

This is a very impressive truth, and might be illustrated to any extent if it were necessary.

EVIL COMMUNICATIONS.

Before discussing the subject of a bad name, a few words must be said on the subject of evil companionships. There is scarcely a subject which gives considerate parents so much trouble, and which is so full of interest to the young. Society of some kind is a necessity.

Alexander Selkirk, in his "Solitude," is most naturally made to say:

> "Oh tell me that I yet have a friend,
> Though a friend I am never to see."

A man closely imprisoned is said to have formed such an attachment to a mouse that he was almost heartbroken when it was taken away. In another instance, a prisoner gratified the social instinct by loving a toad. There never was a more unnatural character than St. Simon Stylites living alone in his pillar of stone. Man to be happy must have some kind of companionship.

Sir John Malcolm, in his "Sketches of Persia," quotes the following fable:

"One day, as I was in the bath, a friend of mine put into my hand a piece of scented clay. I took it and said to it, 'Art thou musk or ambergris, for I am charmed with thy perfume?' It answered, 'I was a despicable piece of clay, but I was some time in the company of the rose. The sweet quality of my companion was communicated to me: otherwise I should be only a bit of clay, as I appear to be!'"

That youth is specially favored who is thrown under the influence of good companions. Such society is elevating to all who come within its reach. But when the young are subjected to evil companionships they are in great danger. The conduct of a certain young man was a puzzle to his friends for years. The mystery was that the son of pious parents should pursue an openly wicked course. In due time the mystery was explained by the fact that a man in his father's employ had gained a powerful influence over the boy, inoculating him with a vice which ruined him. This bad beginning was aggravated by other companions, who tempted him to secret indulgence, until at last his wrong-doing could no longer be concealed. He lived and died a proof that "evil communications corrupt good manners."

At any period of life evil companions are dangerous, but especially so in the period of youth. In a certain village there resided a bright, plausible and zealous skeptic. He was a pleasant talker, and communicated his skepticism in the way least calculated to arouse prejudice. He was constantly surrounded with young men and half-grown boys, and before his mischief was suspected he had sent a dozen of these youths adrift on the unlighted sea of skepticism. His bad work is still visible though more than half a century is gone and the bad man has been dead many years.

In some cases a circle of bad boys, or even a single boy, will corrupt a whole school through the channel of companionship. One such scholar can and sometimes does inflict lifelong injuries on companions who, up to that unfortunate time, have been pure in all respects. In this way some have become confirmed skeptics, others have learned to "look on the wine when it is red," and others to go to "her house which is the way to hell, going down to the chambers of death."

Evil companions are more to be dreaded than wild beasts. A young lad was away from home a few months, and during the time became intimate with an infidel, who acquired a great influence over him. That influence was exerted successfully to unsettle the boy's faith in the Bible and Christianity. Before he was a man he could speak of the "cunningly-devised *fables*" of religion.

There are very few who have been ruined by vicious courses whose vices could not be traced back directly to evil companions. No pestilence is so to be dreaded by the young as a vicious comrade, and they should be more on their guard against this danger than against small pox or cholera. Constant contact with such is likely to lead to any kind of sinful and hurtful indulgence. By this process the very serious natural obstacles in the way of using tobacco are overcome, and men are made by this habit as truly slaves as if they were drunkards. In this way persons become drunkards, gamblers and revelers. In this very way thousands of the young every year sacrifice their good character and reputation, and become the miserable possessors of a bad name which will dog them to the grave as surely as their own ever-pursuing shadows.

Scarcely a more important warning can be addressed to the young than this, "*Beware of evil companions.*" If a companion use oaths, abandon his society at once. If he tipple, or if he sneer at the Bible and religion, or if he indulge in low anecdotes or vile conversation, or if he even *hint* the vilest temptation, flee from him as you would from a poisonous serpent seeking to enfold you in his deadly coils. Pray to God to save you from evil companions, for they often seduce their victims to destruction before their deadly intentions are suspected. "Blessed is the man that walketh not in the counsel of the ungodly, nor standeth in the way of sinners, nor sitteth in the seat of the scornful." "My son, if sinners entice thee, consent thou not. . . . . Walk not in the way with them, refrain thy foot from their path." "A companion of fools shall be destroyed."

He who would preserve his good name must remember that "evil communications corrupt good manners."

CHAPTER X.

UPWARD AIMS.

WE are liable to present a wrong motive to the young by endeavoring to inspire them with that sort of ambition which is the offspring of selfishness and pride. And yet it is right to make up one's mind to excel in every lawful undertaking. An old maxim tells us that "the archer who would hit the moon must aim at the sun." This thought has its applications to all the pursuits and positions of life. We should do the very best we can in whatever situation we may be, and this is to aim upward.

What are some of the good results likely to flow from having upward aims?

IT MAKES A PERSON ECONOMICAL OF TIME.

To waste time is to be guilty of a fault which may be fatal to success in any undertaking; the practical use of time in large measure accounts for the successes and failures of people in life.

There is a man who has acquired a property worth several thousand dollars, while several of his neighbors who began with fairer prospects than himself own nothing. His time was carefully filled up with labor, to gratify his resolution "to better his situation." In the summer he would cultivate his garden and little farm before and after the regular working-hours, thus saving his day's work and feeding his family by his work at times when his neighbors were resting. The late Colonel —— was a man of very general information, and had read as large a number of books as many men of leisure, although he was carrying on an extensive and harassing business. His book was laid where he could take it up without loss of time if he had a few minutes of leisure. In this way he secured hours every week for reading which would have been lost but for his noble upward aim.

The late Dr. Hildreth of Marietta, while in the midst of an extensive practice, kept up with the general literature of the day. Every valuable history, every new work on geology, chemistry, mineralogy, and other books of worth he read carefully, without interfering with the demands of his profession. Dr. V. of Johnsonburg has an extensive country practice, and yet there are few men who have read more books than he. He keeps up with his professional literature; has read the works of every modern historian of any note —Macaulay, Prescott, Bancroft, Motley, Neander, Schaff; he has read a large number of theological books and commentaries. "He is a well-read man," as the saying is. And how do these physicians accomplish so much in the face of such difficulties? They both rise so early as to get an hour or two for their favorite occupation before breakfast, and the book in hand is so placed that they can employ any leisure moments during the day.

If a young man has a will to better his condition, he will show it in his economy of time; and if he have this quality, he has one grand element of success in life.

Included in this item is *industry,* for a person cannot be economical of time and yet not be industrious.

WATCHING FOR OPPORTUNITIES.

This habit of mind *gives a person a practical* and *sagacious watchfulness for special opportunities of success.* Not many years ago a poor boy might have been seen in a certain village. He was animated with a determination to "rise in the world." At school he was on the alert to do the best he could. If he ranked a pile of wood, or worked in some one's garden, or ran to do an errand, the great resolution to rise in the world kept him prompt in performing present duty, and watchful for anything better. Hence, from an errand-boy he became the clerk of a country store. Having established his character there, he was ready to be advanced to a higher post in a city establishment. Here his promptness and energy soon gained for him the confidence of his employers, made him indispensable to them. In due time he became a partner, and at last "the head of the house." Had it not been for his determination to rise, he would have slept through the golden opportunities of success, instead of improving them as they offered.

Success in any pursuit is usually the result of determined and watchful effort, and when a young man aims to do something worthy, and to rise in the world, he will eagerly watch for that

> "Tide in the affairs of men
> Which, taken at the flood, leads on to fortune."

IT ALSO FURNISHES AN OBJECT TO BE ATTAINED.

We are so constituted that we accomplish more when seeking a definite object than when we work at random. Suppose a traveler listlessly set out on his journey in the morning, neither thinking nor caring whether he accomplished twenty or forty miles before night. The day will pass without his doing much. But suppose in the evening he learns from his landlord that a certain town is forty miles distant, and he says, "I can easily drive to such a tavern, twelve miles, to breakfast. By one o'clock I can be at such a village, twenty miles farther on, to dinner, and at sunset I can be at the end of the proposed day's journey." He works to fulfill a *plan*.

A pastor may start from his house without a definite plan before him as to where he will go and whom he will visit, and he will not be likely to do as much as if he were to say, "Here are so many families, and I will visit them to-day."

It is indispensable to success to have something ahead which is in our estimation desirable. Take the case of a boy in a public school. By trial he has found himself able to comprehend the principles of arithmetic and grammar. His memory and imagination aid him in studying geography. From his "reading books" he obtains a few tastes of history, eloquence, philosophy and poetry, and these create a hunger for an education. Perhaps the clergyman or lawyer of the village visits the school and casually tells the scholars how *he* obtained an education, and that if any boy here really desires to get an education, he can do it. That poorly-clad boy says to himself, "I will have it." That purpose in his heart will make a new being of him. His powers are strung to get all that he can from his present limited opportunities, and in due time he can teach others in the common school. Perhaps for some service rendered he finds himself able to buy a Latin grammar, and he begins to do what he can in it. It may take fifteen years to get an education, as he may be obliged to teach one year to gain the means of studying the next year, and yet he will come through the struggle a noble man, and will take a high place in society. Had he not been animated with noble upward aims he never could have achieved such success. His destiny turned on this single resolution, to rise in this particular way.

IT INVIGORATES THE FACULTIES.

Some years ago there was a young man at work cutting and polishing gravestones in a certain establishment in Cincinnati. In carving the various devices common on monuments he displayed a ready talent, and that not merely imitating the designs of others, but in drawing original designs. His success in these undertakings stimulated him to attempt to make models of men well known in the city, in which he succeeded remarkably for a novice. All this while he was agitated with the questions, "Am I always to be a gravestone cutter? Is there no way by which I may become an artist in some higher sphere?" Such self-questionings and such upward aims took him to Italy and won for him the fame of the first living sculptor in the world.

If a young man wishes to do anything worthy, he must have a definite object before him to be attained. This is one of the most important rssults of having an upward aim.

It exerts a surprising influence on all the physical,

mental and moral faculties to have a worthy upward aim. The consciousness of accomplishing something noble is very exhilarating, especially if serious obstacles are to be overcome. A few years ago a young lad resolved that he would get an education. He had no means of his own and could look for very little from his friends. He set himself manfully at his work. Occasionally in the earlier stages of his education he found opportunities to earn some money by working at nights, on Saturdays and during vacations. He was not dainty as to the kind of work, if it were "honest and would pay." He was ready to saw up a wood-pile or copy a legal instrument, or to do anything that came to hand. When he studied he did it with his whole mind, and when he worked he did it with energy. There was animation in all his conduct at the wood-pile, in his study and in his class-room. When he gave you his "good-morning" his voice had a cheery tone, which showed what a noble upward aim was doing for him. For years he encountered very serious difficulties in his course, but all his faculties seemed to grow strong by resistance. At last he brought his diploma home and put it in his mother's hands. His upward aim had given animation, force and hopefulness to all his faculties, and here was the pleasing proof of success.

In contrast with him was another boy who professed a desire to get an education. He began his course, and soon came to difficulties. It was not long before it became evident that he had no higher aim than to find an easier path through life than that of the farmer or mechanic. His aim was *to shun difficulty and labor.* A difficult problem in arithmetic or a hard sentence in the Latin Reader had no charms for him, and was usually passed over with some insincere excuse to his teacher. As for obtaining the means of education by "eating the bread of carefulness," by early rising and energetic use of his time in some remunerative employment, he could not think of it. In fact, his pursuits soon became irksome. He was attentive to his books only by "fits and starts." He fell behind his class. Any pleasure excursion of young people would easily tempt him from his books. In due time he sunk back to his original level, having lost the respect and confidence of those who had hoped better things of him. The main defect seemed to be the want of an intention to accomplish some worthy object.

And lest these remarks be misunderstood to

mean that the young can have no worthy upward aim unless they resolve to leave some lowly but honorable calling for one more honorable in popular esteem, let it be said that this noble aim upward may be shown *in any honest position or sphere.* Take the case of a young man trained to work on a farm. He was not remarkable for his proficiency in his studies. And yet whilst in school there was a noble way with him which indicated his design to act his part well. When he made a profession of religion he did it heartily, and his conduct showed his sincerity. He was prompt in duty, and his life seemed to say to those about him as Moses said to Hobab, "Come thou with us, and we will do thee good." He was a lover of the gospel, and wished to give it to others. When the collection for foreign or home missions or the Bible society was made, people were surprised to learn, in spite of his endeavors to hide the fact, that he always had five or ten dollars laid up for that cause. He is a plain farmer and his hands are as hard as horn. He owns a farm of a hundred acres. Every rail is in place, the barns and out-houses are in fine repair, his garden is neat, and around his house you see the running rose and honeysuckle. His home is a very happy one. It is a privilege to see his family assembled for worship. That man has been moved as really by a noble upward aim as the one who gained a liberal education, and he has been as successful.

The humblest person in the humblest position may aim upward and achieve this great success of doing the best thing possible. Such a course would shed light into many a dwelling now darkened by sheer listlessness and indifference, and would impart the animation of hope to many who are sunk in despondency. If we carefully watch the conduct of young men who frequent saloons, spend their evenings in the unprofitable associations of the store or bar-room, or in low and degrading pleasures, and ask the reason why they can submit to such a waste of time and risk the danger of attending such society, we shall find that this conduct may be traced in part at least to their lack of a purpose in life. They are not animated by an intention to do something good and noble. Supply that lack, and it will drive them away from these places of temptation and change the complexion of their lives. In truth, any young man is in danger of ruin who is not under the influence of some worthy upward aim.

CHAPTER XI.

THE NOBLEST AIM.

THE boy who aspired after money in order that he might buy a comfortable home for his mother had a nobler aim than the boy who sought after wealth merely to better his own condition. How much nobler the aims of the philanthropist Howard and of the unselfish Florence Nightingale than those which inspired Cromwell and Napoleon! Sir Humphrey Davy aimed to provide the miners of England with a "safety lamp" as a means of saving them from the terrible explosions to which they were exposed. Jenner sought a way to check the ravages of small pox, and at last presented to his fellow-men the blessing of *vaccination*. Watt aimed to harness the power of steam and compel it to become a mighty worker for man. Fulton and Stephenson aimed to apply steam to the moving of boats and land carriages. How much nobler are such aims than those which animate the mere conqueror or amasser of wealth! It is easy to perceive the great difference there is among even worthy aims.

What is the noblest aim? Does it imply some striking result that shall dazzle the world? The tubular bridge over the Menai Straits is one of grandest achievements of man, and the world extols the name of Stephenson, who built it. To convey an army over the Alps with all the munitions of war, as Napoleon did by the St. Bernard and as Suwarrow did by St. Gothard, is an enterprise so difficult, so vast, so brilliant, that we look at it with profound admiration. To make and lay down in the ocean separating the Old World and New a magnetic cable, and through it communicate messages from America to Europe, was an achievement that excited the nations with delight, and it seemed as if the very floods clapped their hands. We instinctively applaud any great achievement, whether it be the cutting a tunnel through a mountain, spanning the Niagara with a bridge capable of bearing the heaviest railway trains, conducting the exodus of a nation of bondmen out of Egypt, the deliverance of a people from a foreign master, or any other great achievement. With thrilling interest we mention the names of Moses, David, Cromwell, William the Silent, Washington, Watt, Newton, Daguerre, Morse, and those great men who have done great things in the world.

Does the nobler aim one can have imply some splendid achievement like those just mentioned? If it does, then it is evident that only one in a million can have such an upward aim. The masses of people are not endowed with natural gifts fitting them for the accomplishment of such deeds. The men sufficiently distinguished to be named in history are very few. Those who are forgotten are very many. It is a very singular fact that in Rollin's "Ancient History of the Egyptians, Carthaginians, Assyrians, Babylonians, Medes and Persians, Grecians, Romans," etc., covering a period of more than two thousand years, there were only about two thousand names of sufficient note to be mentioned in a copious index! Of these names very many are not familiar even to scholars; to the masses of people most of even these historical names are unknown. The hundreds of millions who dwelt on the earth during that period are entirely forgotten. It would be mockery then to counsel young men to aspire to such a notoriety as Alexander, Napoleon or Newton had, knowing that not one in a hundred millions can reach it.

Every young man should make the best use of his talents, carefully cultivating and invigorating them as his opportunities admit, but let it be marked that no mere mental attainment, however brilliant, can constitute the highest aim to be sought. This implies the exercise of the noblest faculties—those which ally man to God. As a moral being, man is created in the image of God. From this estate he has fallen, and one of the saddest evidences of his fall is found in his low aims. He lives to himself, he seeks his own gratification, and "God is not in all his thoughts." If he follow the path of conquest, the love of self impels him. If he explore the secret places of the earth for the treasures there concealed, the same selfish motive inspires him. If he apply the power of his mind to explain the mysteries of nature in the heavens and the earth and the waters under the earth, he is not moved thereto by a desire to glorify God. He may call it the love of science, or the love of nature, or the love of an honorable name among men, yet the motive is one that seeks to minister to his self-gratification. Even in the less conspicuous, but not less important walks of life, which centre in *home,* by nature man does not rise above some species of selfishness. Many a character which the world has pronounced noble when tried by the law of God has shrunk into the most intense selfishness.

TWO CASES IN POINT.

Some years ago a young man was pursuing his studies in college with great success. He was not a pious man, but his deportment was that of a gentleman among his companions. He was not obsequious in his attentions to "the Faculty," but he was a manly observer of the rules of the institution. He had too much good sense to contrast his conduct with that of inconsistent professors, but there were persons who drew the contrast in colors sometimes quite unfavorable to religion. With not a little emphasis you would hear such ask, "In what respect can religion better the conduct or character of ——?"

That question was to be answered. During the winter of his junior year the college was pervaded with powerful religious influences. The young men walked quietly through the halls as if on holy ground. The sounds of song and laughter were not heard. The chapel exercises were marked with profound solemnity, and go into what room you would, you would find signs of God's presence. Scores were rejoicing in hope, but, strange as it may seem, no one had felt at liberty to approach this moral young man on this great theme which engrossed the attention of all others. One evening an intimate friend went to his room to ask him to seek the Lord, but was astounded to find himself rudely commanded to leave the room, and never again to open his lips to him on so hateful a subject! The model student was in an agony of conviction, and raged like a lion in the toils. We all wondered at the sight, but as the Spirit of God tore away the coverings with which the deceitful and desperately wicked heart had concealed itself not merely from our knowledge, but from that of the young man himself, he seemed to himself to be a very devil in wickedness. All his prided goodness had vanished, and in place of that he saw that he had never done one holy act in all his life, because he had been moral and kind and decorous from entirely selfish motives. He had never aimed to glorify and love God. Hence his rage and confusion and shame as the Spirit of God compelled

him to look into his polluted heart, up to that time like an unlighted dungeon full of loathsome reptiles and reeking with filth. The most profane and openly wicked of his companions seemed to him saints in the comparison. In a few days he found peace with God through our Lord Jesus Christ; and as the marvelous change in him was seen, there was found no scoffer to ask what benefit a change of heart could be to so moral a young man. His life was one controlled by motives and aims entirely new to him.

Very similar to this was the case of a young man who had lost his father. The responsibility of providing for the family fell on him. It was a trying position, which required him to abandon a favorite occupation, and to engage in pursuits which were not to his taste. There were some peculiar perplexities which attended his discharge of duty, and yet no one ever heard him name the sacrifice of position and inclination he had made, nor utter a fretful complaint at the annoyances which he had to encounter. People applauded his manliness and his dutiful affection to those dependent on him. To these praises he was not deaf, and they ministered to the vanity of his deceived heart. As he afterward admitted, he had

built a firm hope of heaven on his self-righteousness. In what could he be better? What more could he do even if he were professedly religious? Would he be more honest in business?—more attentive to his widowed mother and her children?—more exemplary as a supporter of the church, and an observer of the Sabbath?—more worthy as a citizen?

The time came for God to try his foundation, and he might have described the trial in the words of Job: "I was at ease, but he hath broken me asunder. He hath also taken me by my neck and shaken me to pieces, and set me up for his mark. . . . . He breaketh me with breach upon breach. He runneth upon me like a giant."[1] During a season of revival his mind was disturbed with the fear that his hope of heaven was not built on a sure foundation. He believed that a great many *wicked* people needed to undergo great spiritual change, but for a time he resisted and resented the idea that *he* needed such a change. But the more he thought of the claims of God, not only to a perfect outward conformity to his laws, but to such a state of heart as that supreme love to God shall be the great motive of

[1] Job xvi. 12–14.

all action, the more unsettled did he become. His former hopes were fled, and he was left very unhappy. The conviction had taken firm hold of his mind that he had never done one act from a desire to glorify God. He had been caring for his widowed mother and her children because upon the whole such a course would give himself the most profit and satisfaction. He had put up with the many annoyances of his situation because it won for him so good a name among his acquaintances. Had he shunned all responsibility and cast off his helpless charge to get rid of trouble, he could not have been more truly selfish than in his present course. What cared he about *God?* How little had the love of God to do with conduct which was in itself admirable!

As he was thus taught of the Spirit, it surprised no Christian of experience to hear this admirable son, this attentive brother, this model citizen, saying, with heart-breaking grief, as if he were the chief of sinners, "God, be merciful to me a sinner!" Had he been "before a blasphemer," the change in him could not have been more distinctly visible.

These illustrations will show how entirely selfish a person may be in many of those aims which are deemed noble among men, and which in some cases become a righteousness which supplants the righteousness of Christ. The noblest aim must be inspired by a higher principle than a godless selfishness.

THE QUESTION ANSWERED.

What then *is* the noblest upward aim to the attainment of which we may encourage the young? It is to live and act in all things so as to glorify God and show the love of Christ. Joshua said: "As for me and my house we will serve the Lord," and the Apostle Paul said: "The love of Christ constraineth us."

We admire and applaud those good acts which are done under higher than sordid motives. Some men are brave in rescuing persons from danger in hope of reward; others are no less brave because it wins for them a noble name, and others for the love of God and man. Suppose a case: A poor stranger has been removed to a lonely cabin on yonder hill because he has the small pox. The question is put to three men, "Will you go and take care of this man?" The first one says, "I am willing to risk the danger for five dollars a day." The second one says, "I will take care of him because in so doing I shall bring upon myself the admiration of others as a brave and humane man." The third says, "I will take care of him because he is my brother and to show my love of Jesus."

We would not blame the first one for naming his price, nor would we think of applauding his goodness any more than we would the goodness of any other laborer naming the wages for which he is willing to work. Judged by human standards, the conduct of the second one was far nobler than that of the first. *Fame* is a word that sounds sweetly in the human ear, and for it many have risked death in the most awful forms. Yet the difference between the one willing to nurse the small-pox patient for so much *money*, and the one who is willing to do it for so much fame, is not so great as might at first appear. In each case the aspiration was purely selfish, and the difference in the rewards demanded for the services could be traced to a difference in taste.

But the third one was willing to go to the lonely cabin on the hilltop, spend tedious days and nights alone with the sufferer, handle him in his loathesomeness, breathe the infected atmosphere, and stay with him until the disease had spent itself, not for the love of money, nor for the love of fame, but for the love he bore to that sufferer as his brother man and to Jesus as his Saviour. He would do it if there were no reward in money, or if his conduct were to remain a profound secret. The love of Christ constrained him. There was such a cabin in which once lay such a sufferer in horrible loneliness and loathesomeness, away from his mother and his wife, and a young Christian man nursed him with the tenderness of a woman until he died. He neither asked nor received reward, nor did he apparently once think of fame. The motive which impelled him was the love of the sufferer and the love of Jesus. The almost infinite superiority of this motive to all others we instinctively admit.

Is this answer merely *ideal*, that the noblest of all upward aims is to love and act in all things under the impelling power of the desire to glorify God and love Jesus? The most sordid men admit the beauty and superiority of the motive, and yet very many doubt whether such a motive can exist except as the dream of some enthusiast. They deny the existence of such a motive as a practical and attainable reality. It is some gain to have this heavenly *ideal* admitted even in *theory.* Let us see whether it does not exist in *fact.*

MOSES AND PAUL.

A case from the Old Testament and one from the New will prove that the fact here asserted has existed.

A young man, one of an enslaved and despised race, had become the adopted son of a princess in a powerful and learned nation. Endowed with a surpassing genius and the highest advantages of education, he became the most noted youth in the kingdom. His mental faculties were perfectly trained and his stores of knowledge were vast. In addition to these qualities, he was fitted by nature and education to command men. There was no position next to the king which he might not have attained, there was no wealth which he might not have hoped to gain, and no worldly pleasure or good which was not within his reach. His own people were in bondage, and were both despised and dreaded by their oppressors. To be numbered with them was to fall from his position in the court, and apparently to sacrifice every worldly prospect.

Had MOSES been governed by worldly and selfish motives, he would have chosen the pleasures, honors and rewards of remaining in so enviable a position as that to which he had attained. He certainly would not have chosen to suffer affliction with the people of God rather than enjoy the pleasures of sin for a season. A worldly mind never prefers duty and affliction to the highest worldly prosperity. Look at that young man deliberately refusing to be called the son of Pharaoh's daughter, joining himself to the enslaved and despised Israelites, going into a long and apparently hopeless exile, and you see a very remarkable fact disclosed. Is it asked, What was the motive leading him to such a choice? It was faith in God, and his desire to please God, for "he endured as seeing Him who is invisible." No ordinary motive will account for the choice.

If Moses was the greatest man mentioned in Old Testament history, *Paul* is the greatest in the New. There dwelt a breadth, depth, greatness and force in this man which have never been surpassed. These were not miraculous attributes, but they belonged to him as part of his nature. His intellect was gifted with most keen perceptions and most vigorous reasoning faculties. After the crucifixion of Jesus, whom he never saw before his conversion, and after that first great awakening was turning Jerusalem and the world upside down, this man alone of the enemies of Christ had sufficient sagacity to perceive that the very existence of his own devoutly believed Judaism depended on the destruction of the new religion, and that the object could not be attained by any half-way measures. His nature was earnest and passionate, and when he was convinced that the new religion must be exterminated, he set himself to do it with all his might. His burning earnestness pervaded the ranks of his friends. He was the chieftain in this war, and his force sent spies into every house in Jerusalem to discover and drag to prison all the followers of Jesus. No language can be more historically true or forcible than his own in describing himself at this period: "I verily thought with myself that *I ought to do* many things contrary to the name of Jesus of Nazareth. Which thing I also *did* in Jerusalem; and many of the saints did I shut up in prison, having received authority from the chief priests; and when they were put to death I gave my voice against them. And I punished them oft in every synagogue, and *compelled them to blaspheme* (Jesus); and being exceedingly mad against them, I persecuted them even unto strange cities." The significant remark of the historian is: "As for Saul, he made havoc of the Church, entering into every house, and haling (dragging violently) men and women, committed them to prison." And when the Lord bade Ananias go and baptize Saul, the good man was in doubt whether the conversion of such a man was possible, for he exclaimed in amazement, "Lord, I have heard by many of this man, how much evil he hath done to thy saints at Jerusalem." Saul was not acting insincerely. He was as sincere in his belief that Jesus was an impostor as he was after his conversion that Jesus was the Messiah. He fully believed himself to be right and that he was doing God's will. He "was zealous toward God," and said, "I have lived in all good conscience before God until this day." He was the great man of the Jewish Church and nation, and his magnificent gifts as a scholar, a thinker and leader were rapidly acquiring for him the highest worldly honors.

Besides these considerations, he had in the most public manner committed himself in his opposition to the religion and saints of Jesus. He had assailed both in the most positive modes. Weak minds easily change their opinions and courses of action, but nothing is more displeasing to a highly-endowed mind than the suspicion of inconsistency or vacillation. It was not surprising that the artful and low-minded Simon Magus should renounce his impostures and receive baptism as a professed convert to Christianity. But nothing less than the power of God could overcome the profound convictions and pride of position with which such a one as Saul was guarded as in a moral Gibraltar.

No worldly and selfish motive can account for the conversion of this man and his subsequent life, since all the motives of his character resisted any change. He sacrificed cherished convictions and associations, honors and rewards, and took to himself indescribable persecutions, sorrows and hardships.

And what was the noble aim of his soul leading him to count all things but loss? It was to love, serve and win Christ. In a most remarkable manner he describes the mainspring which moved the machinery of his life: "Whether we be beside ourselves it is to God. . . . . The love of Christ constraineth us." "For me to live is Christ." "Christ is all in all."

Admit the existence of this noblest of all aims, to glorify God and show forth the love of Jesus, and the conversion and life of Paul, with all their attendant worldly discomforts, sacrifices and sufferings, are explained. An ignorant person might look at an ocean steamer sailing in the teeth of the tempest and the tide. He sees simply the great ship overcoming opposition, and yet he knows not what the power is that impels it. But to one who knows the power of steam, the movement of the ship against tide and tempest is a result which he can appreciate as he descends into the hold, sees the huge furnaces and boilers, the cylinder and shafts by which the ship is driven "whithersoever the governor listeth." It is even so with the life of the Apostle Paul. The love of Jesus as its grand and impelling force will be a cause sufficient to account for every sacrifice he made and every suffering he endured. This cause is sufficient to account for the result, and no other is.

OTHER ILLUSTRATIONS.

From uninspired history other examples of the highest aim may be selected.

At a retired country parsonage on the banks of the Connecticut, in the year of our Lord 1703, there was born a child who was destined to become one of the greatest of men. His mind was directed to religious things when he was a child, and he was converted whilst in college in 1720. He entered Yale when he was twelve years old, and graduated before he was seventeen with the highest honors. Even then, such was the vigor of his intellect that he read "Locke on the Human Understanding" with the keenest pleasure. Endowed with marvelous reasoning faculties, his imagination was not less marvelous. He had the gift of abstraction so that he could bend all the forces of his mighty intellect to the solution of any problem in metaphysics or theology, and from such rugged wrestlings with the difficult he could go on strong wings up to the very gates of paradise or down to the bottomless pit of eternal horrors, describing each in the language of essential poetry. In the opinion of Dr. Chalmers he was "the greatest of theologians, combining . . . . the profoundly intellectual with the devotedly spiritual and sacred, and realizing in his own person a most rare yet most beautiful harmony between the simplicity of the Christian pastor on the one hand, and on the other all the strength and prowess of a giant in philosophy. If we consider his originality and force of genius impressing itself as distinctly on theology as did the genius of Bacon on philosophy or Newton on astronomy, or if we regard him as a preacher whose arguments, imagination and intense earnestness were irresistible, we may conclude that few if any greater men have been born in America." This meek New England divine was President Edwards, one of the lights of the world.

This man subjected his extraordinary gifts to that noblest aim which prompted him to live so as to glorify God and show his love for Christ. When yet a very young man he "resolved never to do, be or suffer anything in soul or body, less or more, but what tends to the glory of God;" "Never to act as if I were any way my own, but entirely and altogether God's;" "Never to do anything but duty, and then do it willingly and cheerfully as unto the Lord;" and "To live with all my might while I do live."

As Stephenson sketched on paper his drafts of the great tubular bridge, and as the architect of St. Peter's sketched his splendid conception of that famous cathedral, so did Edwards in his "Resolutions" sketch his own life as he desired it to be. Among these seventy resolutions we find in those just quoted the main principles which were to give character and life to all the rest. He was resolved to live with all his might to declare the glory of God and the love of Christ. How far did he realize his own resolutions?

This idea pervaded both his meditations and actions. "Looking upon the sky and clouds there came into his mind an unspeakably sweet sense of the glorious majesty and grace of God. .... God's excellency, his wisdom, his purity and love seemed to appear in everything." Whilst in New York he had such views of holiness as were wonderful. "It appeared to me to be of a sweet, pleasant, charming, serene, calm nature, which brought an inexpressible purity, brightness, peacefulness and ravishment to the soul." "He had the greatest delight in the Holy Scriptures." "His soul seemed like such a little white flower as we see in the spring of the year, low and humble on the ground, opening its bosom to receive the pleasant beams of the sun's glory, rejoicing as it were in a calm rapture, diffusing around a sweet fragrancy, standing peacefully and lovingly in the midst of other flowers round about, all in like manner opening their bosoms to drink in the light of the sun." At one time he spake of the wonderful, great, full, pure and sweet grace and love of Christ, as of his desire to "be full of Christ alone, to love him with a pure and holy love." "This constant solemn converse with God made his face to shine before others."

If we follow this man from his study to the pulpit, and from his meditations to his life, we find him living with all his might to glorify God and love Christ. His sermons, his words, his actions, were all full of this glorious upward aim. In his seclusion the love of Christ was, like fire on the altar, never extinguished, and in his actions the same love constrained him to live not unto himself, but unto Him who died for him and rose again. This was the high and noble aim which he constantly set before him.

Such was the elder Edwards, one of the greatest of uninspired men and one of the holiest of those who "have obtained a good report through faith."

It would be an easy task to fill many pages with examples quite similar and scarcely less conspicuous. Such an one was David Brainerd. Once when among the Indians he said: "I cared not how or where I lived, or what hardships I went through, so that I could but gain souls to Christ." "All my desire was the conversion of the heathen, and all my hope was in God." "All my desire is to glorify God."

Richard Baxter declared his "resolution to be fixed to live and labor for eternity," and that "the ministerial work must be carried on purely for God and the salvation of souls, not for any private ends of our own." Henry Martyn unfolded the secret of his wonderful life when he said:

"I all on earth forsake,
Its wisdom, fame and power,
And Him my only portion make,
My shield and tower."

CHAPTER XII.

HOW SHALL I BECOME A CHRISTIAN?

MANY are ready to admit the excellence and beauty of the principle just illustrated, that to act under the controlling desire to glorify God and to love Christ is the noblest upward aim. They appreciate the examples of such good men as are named in the eleventh chapter of the Epistle to the Hebrews, the apostles and martyrs, and those who in every age have been enabled to cast into "the deepest, fathomless part of the ocean . . . . that burdensome millstone about their neck—I mean SELF, showing it no mercy, for Christ, for his cross, for his people, counting all things but loss."[1] But the difficulty is of a practical nature. They are conscious that they are not under the control of so lofty an aim. Nay, they see that SELF is the central motive, the im-

[1] J. W. Alexander's Sac. Discourses, p. 366.

pelling power which shapes and controls their actions. And now they make an effort to cast out *self* and to enthrone the love of Christ in their hearts, but find themselves in a dilemma which may be described in the words of an apostle: "To will is present with me: but how to perform that which is good, I find not."[1] It seems to them very much like one who relishes one kind of food, but loathes another, resolving that he will change his tastes so as to love what he loathes and to loathe what he loves; or like one who has been addicted to some bad habit, and resolves that he will not even in thought admit the supremacy of this habit. Such a one finds that it is one thing "*to will*," but quite another thing "*to do*." In other words, they may resolve to do what in fact they find themselves unable to do. The inability is not such as to excuse them as blameless, but it has two phases which illustrate its power. In the first place, the unconverted, but awakened, find a strong disposition in their moral natures to act solely under the direction of selfish motives. And in the second place, they find either no disposition, or at least a very feeble disposition, to enthrone the love of Christ

[1] Rom. vii. 18.

as the governing principle of their natures. That is, they find a very strong disposition to love self supremely, which God has forbidden, and no disposition to love God and Christ supremely, as God has commanded.

It has been stated as a fact that a man once fell into a kind of cataleptic state which was marked by this peculiarity, that whilst there was not a sign of life which his friends could discover, he was entirely conscious of what was taking place about him. He could hear what they said, and he knew that they were preparing to bury him. He desired to speak, but his tongue would not obey him; to move, but his limbs continued rigid; to show some sign that he was not dead, but his whole body remained as cold and immovable as death. His will had for the time lost all control of the body, and he found himself unable to do what he greatly desired to do.

Many an awakened sinner has found himself in a somewhat similar situation. He perceives the right, but finds it exceedingly hard to do it. He sees that God commands him to love the Lord his God with all his heart, and he feels that he ought to make this love the controlling motive of his life and actions. He knows that now he does not do this, and that he is guilty of a very offensive and dangerous sin. He resolves to cease to act from selfish motives and begin to act from the purpose to love God. But his resolution to do this no more brings about the desired result than the man's resolution to show his friends that he was not dead. He finds that his whole nature is pervaded with the most positive and inveterate selfishness and an utter indisposition to adopt the love of God as the ruling motive. If he intelligently scrutinize the workings of his spiritual nature, he will come to some knowledge of the divine saying, "The heart is deceitful above all things, and desperately wicked."

We have a confirmation of this statement in the attempt of awakened men to "make themselves better." One has been profane, and he resolves to correct this evil habit. He may cease swearing, but the heart is unchanged. Another has been an undutiful son, a reckless member of the household. Now that his mind is uneasy, he determines that he will be very kind and obedient to his parents and exemplary to his family. And yet he is conscious that his reformation is only external, and such as it is, it is very difficult to maintain it. Another one has been engaged in some immoral business or has been dishonest in some lawful calling. So soon as he is awakened he sets about an outward reformation, and yet, even though he accomplish it, he is not satisfied. Another who is moral in his conduct, but a neglecter of religious privileges and duties, aims to pay more respect and attention to the Bible, the Sabbath and public worship. And yet in many such cases people wonder that their religious trouble does not cease, and that they are not full of happiness.

Quite similar is the experience of awakened sinners who have been educated in any anti-Christian religion. Hundreds of Roman Catholics have been awakened, and they have asked, "What shall we do?" They acknowledge their sins and resolve on reformation. They ask their spiritual advisers for counsel, and readily undergo some mortifying penances. Some have made large pecuniary sacrifices, and have done many things to find peace with God. Yet their penances have not brought the desired peace. They have found it far easier to accomplish a painful pilgrimage than to "make them a new heart," to pay money and make sacrifices than to exterminate selfishness and to love God with all the heart.

This is a real difficulty.

THE NEW HEART.

There must be a great moral change, and this fact is declared in various ways in the Scriptures. "Create in me a clean heart, O God, and renew a right spirit within me."[1] "Make you a new heart and a new spirit."[2] "I will put a new spirit within you, and I will take the stony heart out of their flesh, and will give them a heart of flesh."[3] "Verily, verily, I say unto thee, Except a man be born again he cannot see the kingdom of God."[4] "If any man be in Christ, he is a new creature."[5]

The nature of this change has been hinted at in the discussion of the question, "What is the noblest aim?" It is a change in the governing purpose of the soul. The unrenewed man loves himself supremely, and does all that he does under the constraining influence of this self-love. He does not ask himself, when forming and executing his plans, Will this and that course of con-

[1] Ps. li. 10. [2] Ezek. xviii. 31. [3] Ezek. xi. 19.
[4] John iii. 3, 5, 7. [5] 2 Cor. v. 17.

duct please God? or, Can I by this action or this self-denial glorify God? "God is not in all his thoughts."[1] The divine command is perfectly plain. "The Lord our God is one Lord, and thou shalt love the Lord thy God with all thine heart, and with all thy soul, and with all thy might."[2] "Whether therefore ye eat or drink, or whatsoever ye do, do all to the glory of God."[3] When a moral being makes the love of God the supreme motive of all his actions, the reason for doing one thing and abstaining from doing another, then is he a friend of God and has "this testimony, that he pleases God."[4] The angels thus love God, and all holy beings are thus constrained by this mighty motive. They do not need a *new* heart, and need not ask God to *create* in them a *clean* heart.

But every descendant of Adam has fallen from this state. "They are corrupt, they have done abominable works, there is none that doeth good. The Lord looked down from heaven to see if there were any that did understand and seek God. They are all gone aside, they are altogether become filthy. There is none that doeth good, no,

[1] Ps. x. 4. [2] Deut. vi. 4, 5.
[3] 1 Cor. x. 31. [4] Heb. xi. 5.

not one."[1] These words are invested with double authority by being quoted by the Apostle Paul to prove the whole world guilty before God.[2]

What does this mean? The young man whom Jesus loved had not a suspicion that he fell into the common condemnation pronounced on all mankind in these and similar declarations, for when Jesus named the requirements usually included in the second table of the Law, he said: "All these things have I kept from my youth up: what lack I yet?"[3]

The Scriptures declare all to be sinners who have corrupted their way before God. Let us suppose a young man whose reputation among men is unblemished to ask some such questions as these: "Do you mean to say that I do not love my parents and treat them with becoming respect? or that I am an unkind and selfish brother? or that I am no respecter of the rights of my neighbors? Did you ever hear me curse father or mother? Did you ever see me drunk? Did you ever know me to lie, cheat or steal? If not, what do you mean by saying that *I* am an utterly corrupt sinner before God?"

How many moral young men have allowed

[1] Ps. xiv. 1, 3. [2] Rom. iii. 10–20. [3] Matt. xix. 20.

themselves thus to question the charges made against them in the Bible!

To such a one it might be answered: "You say you love and honor your father and mother. Do you do this because you honor God? You say you are kind to your neighbor and honest in your dealings. Are you kind and honest because in this way you are striving to love God with all your heart? You pursue certain courses in life, you abstain from certain other courses. Do you do this in order that whatsoever you do, you may do all to the glory of God?"

And what can the young man say to these questions but to admit that he has been impelled by no such motive as the love of God?—that in fact he has been as selfish and as regardless of God in his love of his parents and his honesty of life as another son has been in his ill treatment of his parents and his dishonesty of life? So far as *regard to God as the ruling motive of life* is concerned, all the unregenerate occupy a common level. A young man may be as moral in his life as the young man whom Jesus loved, and yet be as really destitute of the love of God as Judas or Herod.

We see what the Scriptures mean by declaring

that all mankind are sinners: they mean that every descendant of Adam is destitute of the love of God as an impelling and controlling motive of action, and that each one has substituted selfishness in heart for the love of God.

What, then, is the new heart, or regeneration, or conversion? What is it to become a Christian?

To cast out selfishness from the heart as a supreme motive of action and to enthrone the love of God in its place—this is to have a new heart, to be regenerate, to become a Christian. *How* this change takes place is a mystery, but the *fact* is as plain as any other fact. "The wind bloweth where it listeth, and thou hearest the sound thereof, but canst not tell whence it cometh, and whither it goeth; so is every one that is born of the Spirit."[1] How the wind blows is a mystery, but the *fact* that it does blow is as evident as any other fact.

To prove that this view of the change when one becomes a Christian is true, we have only to appeal to the Scriptures and to those who have become Christians. Thus the apostle says of man in his unregenerate state: "The carnal mind is enmity against God; for it is not subject unto the

[1] John iii. 8.

law of God, neither indeed can be."[1] But of himself as a renewed man, one who has a "new heart," he says: "I delight in the law of God after the inward man."[2] "The law of God" is this, "Thou shalt love the Lord thy God with all thy heart," but before the change the "carnal mind" rises in rebellion against this law, but after the change the renewed man delights in this law.

In the gospel Jesus is revealed as the Son of God, and as entitled to equal honor with the Father. Before his conversion Saul was a blasphemer of Jesus, and he compelled others to be blasphemers also.[3] But after his conversion the renewed Paul counted all things but loss that he might win Christ, and moved as steadily and swiftly forward as a planet in her orbit under the constraining love of Christ.[4] Zaccheus was reputed to be "a sinner" before his conversion, and, from his own reference to extortion, may be supposed to have been no exception to the class of which he was one in respect to his selfishness. But after his conversion he gave the half of his goods to the poor, and promised fourfold restitution in every case in which he had "taken any-

[1] Rom. viii. 7.
[2] Rom. vii. 22.
[3] 1 Tim. i. 13; *Acts* xxvi. 11.
[4] Phil. iii. 1-14; 2 Cor. v. 14.

thing from any man by false accusation." The love of Christ had succeeded the love of self as a motive of action.

Ask Augustine, who was in his early life a corrupt and selfish libertine, in what consisted the change he professed to experience, and he will tell you that the love of God as the supreme motive had cast out the love of self. Ask Luther, Calvin, Wesley, Whitefield, Edwards, Brainerd, Henry Martyn, and any other Christians whose piety is as conspicuous as the light, for the motive which inspired their lives before they were converted, and they will tell you that they were supremely devoted to self and regardless of God. But after God made them new creatures they could say: "The love of Christ constraineth us to live not unto ourselves, but unto Him who died for us and rose again."

WHO MAKES THE NEW CREATURE?

The very terms used in the Bible point directly to the power which works this change. Many millions of men have tried to make themselves cease to act selfishly, and instead to act solely from the love of God, and they have found themselves as powerless to effect the change as to raise the dead to life. What volumes of sorrowful experience are contained in that one sentence which describes the vain struggles of awakened sinners!—"Before they would come to Christ they must needs try to make themselves better." Never has a sinner come off victor in an unaided wrestle with the selfishness of his own heart; never has he felt that he alone could kindle on the altar of his selfish heart the pure flame of holy love to God. He has tried, but failed, and if there be no other help, he must perish.

This defines the agency which effects this change. "The Holy Spirit of God"[1] is the only power named in the Bible as regenerating the sinner's heart. Thus our Saviour said to Nicodemus, first in general terms and then in more specific, "Except a man be born *from above* (again), he cannot see the kingdom of God;" "Except a man be born of water and of the SPIRIT, he cannot enter into the kingdom of God. That which is born of the flesh is flesh, and that which is born of the *Spirit* is spirit."[2] These declarations define and restrict the general statement made by the Evangelist John when he speaks of "them that believe on his name" as "born not of blood, nor of the will

[1] Eph. iv. 30. [2] John iii. 3, 5, 6.

of the flesh, nor of the will of man, but of GOD."[1] When Jesus was about to leave the world he promised to send them "another Comforter, that he may abide with you for ever, even the Spirit of truth; . . . . the Holy Ghost whom the Father will send in my name, he shall teach you all things."[2] And when the day of Pentecost was fully come the disciples "were all filled with the Holy Ghost." The words of Peter addressed to the unconverted multitudes which thronged about him were made efficient by this power, so that thousands in agony cried out, "Men and brethren, what shall we do?"[3]

If we examine the history of those marvelous changes which attended the preaching of the apostles and Christians[4] as recorded by Luke, and compare them with the doctrinal statements of the Apostle Paul, we cannot fail to trace them to the mighty power of the Holy Spirit. Thus the apostle bids his brethren not to "grieve the Holy Spirit of God, whereby ye are sealed unto the day of redemption."[5] He also says of them in another connection, "Ye were sealed with that Holy Spirit of promise."[6] The apostle describes

[1] John i. 12, 13. [2] John xiv. 16, 26. [3] Acts ii., *passim*.
[4] Acts viii. 4. [5] Eph. iv. 30. [6] Eph. i. 13.

the agency which converted certain sinners into Christian believers by comparing them to "an epistle of Christ ministered by us, written not with ink, but with the *Spirit of the living God;* not in tables of stone, but in fleshly tables of the heart."[1] He points to the same power in declaring that we are not "sufficient of ourselves to think anything as of ourselves, but our sufficiency is of God."[2] The agency of the Holy Spirit in the conversion and sanctification of sinners is made very prominent in the eighth chapter of Romans, and elsewhere in the apostle's letters. "For as many as are led by the Spirit of God, they are the sons of God."[3] "God hath from the beginning chosen you to salvation through sanctification of the Spirit and belief of the truth."[4] "Not by works of righteousness which we have done, but according to his mercy, he saved us, by the washing of regeneration and renewing of the Holy Ghost."[5]

The only efficient power to regenerate the wicked heart, by casting out selfishness and enthroning the love of God as its constraining motive, is the third person of the triune Godhead, called in the

[1] 2 Cor. iii. 3. [2] 2 Cor. iii. 5. [3] Rom. viii. 14.
[4] 2 Thess. ii. 13. [5] Titus iii. 5.

Scriptures "the Holy Ghost," the "Comforter,"[1] "the Spirit of God,"[2] "the Spirit of the living God,"[3] "the Holy Spirit of God,"[4] "the Spirit,"[5] and "the Holy Spirit."[6]

The particular interest of this statement may be thus illustrated. In proportion to the desirableness of an object to be attained, and the greatness of the difficulties which prevent our attainment of that object, is our satisfaction in finding assistance equal to our wants. Thus a young man fell into a deep well, and was unable to get out. His cries fortunately brought men to his rescue. But another young man was assisting to dig a well. Suddenly he found that the quicksands had fastened his feet, and his situation was rendered the more horrible by the caving of the earth about him. His companions were frightened too much to do anything, and they were afraid to venture down into so dangerous a place. Gradually the earth closed him up in its relentless embrace, while his companions stood horror-stricken at a doom which they had no power to avert. What joy would have been brought to the endangered youth and his friends had some bold,

[1] John xiv. 26. [2] Rom. viii. 9. [3] 2 Cor. iii. 3.
[4] Ephes. iv. 30. [5] Gal. v. 18. [6] 1 Thess. iv. 8.

strong, experienced man appeared at the critical moment to point out a plan and to execute it for his deliverance! The extremity of the danger would have added to the desirableness of a deliverer.

Some years ago a peculiarly insidious and dangerous disease began its ravages in a certain institution. When the physician was called, he pronounced it a disease whose peculiar type was not described in the medical authorities, and one which he had never seen before. Other physicians were called, who came to the same conclusion. Meanwhile, one of the young men, a very gifted student, had died. Another was in the most critical condition. A person in the neighborhood was evidently dying, while a score of students were showing symptoms of the disease. It was a time of alarm, and this alarm was increased by the fact that the physicians were evidently at their wits' end.

In the midst of this panic a physician who was almost an entire stranger to the profession in the region, having recently come there, introduced himself to the doctor in charge, with the request to be allowed to visit these patients with him the next day. The request was granted, and after a very careful examination of the cases the stranger said: "Last winter I had many cases very similar to these, and some of them died, but after various experiments I adopted a particular mode of treatment (which he described), and after that every patient recovered."

The information seemed so sensible, and it was imparted with so much modesty and generosity, that he was requested to aid the regular physician in the management of the cases. It was not a week before those who were sick showed signs of recovery, and the gloom which overhung the seminary was passing away. The reason was twofold: the danger was great, and the new physician proved himself equal to the task of dealing with it.

We have examined that moral disease which is as widely prevalent as the human family. As before the flood, so since in every age, "God saw that the wickedness of man was great in the earth, and that every imagination of the thoughts of his heart was only evil continually."[1] We have traced this disease back to its starting-point. The love of God as the supreme motive of thought, action and life is wanting in "the carnal mind,"[2]

[1] Gen. vi. 5. [2] Rom. viii. 7; Gal. v. 17.

and in place of this we find a supreme selfishness which has usurped the place of God. This selfishness leads each one to live to himself regardless of God; and instead of asking, "How can I please and glorify God?" the great and real question is, "How can I please myself?" This is enmity to God, and is most displeasing to him, and God will render unto them who are guilty of it "indignation and wrath, tribulation and anguish."[1] It is a condition of heart "desperately wicked,"[2] and such a fountain of bitterness cannot send forth at the same place "sweet water and bitter, ... salt water and fresh."[3] Here is the reason which justifies God in saying of the whole human family, "There is none that doeth good, no, not one."[4]

We have seen that this is a most deep-rooted state of heart—a disease which has baffled the skill and power of all human physicians. But it is not only very hard to cure, but it is certain to be attended with the most fatal consequences if it be not cured. The Lord Jesus has made an atonement for our sins, and has made our salvation possible. "It is a faithful saying, and worthy

[1] Rom. ii. 8, 9. [2] Jer. xvii. 9.
[3] James iii. 11, 12. [4] Ps. xiv. 3.

of all acceptation, that Christ Jesus came into the world to save sinners."[1] Yet even this glorious provision for our salvation would be in vain if the Holy Spirit did not take the things of Christ and show them to sinners,[2] "for we are his workmanship, created in Christ Jesus unto good works."[3] It matters not who sows the seed, it is God who giveth the increase,[4] and he does this by pouring out his Spirit upon all flesh,[5] but especially upon "them who shall be heirs of salvation."[6]

"Can aught beneath a power divine
The stubborn will subdue?
'Tis thine, eternal Spirit, thine,
To form the heart anew.

* * * * *

"Oh change these wretched hearts of ours,
And give them life divine;
Then shall our passions and our powers,
Almighty God, be thine!"

HUMAN AGENCIES.

It has been proved that the Holy Spirit is the only power that creates the sinner's heart anew. Some thoughtful mind may inquire, *What then*

[1] 1 Tim. i. 15. [2] John xvi. 15. [3] Eph. ii. 10.
[4] 1 Cor. iii. 6, 7. [5] Joel ii. 28. [6] Heb. i. 14.

has the sinner to do but sit still and see the salvation of God?

The Apostle Paul has presented this subject under the figure of sowing seed. "I have planted, Apollos watered, but God gave the increase. So then neither is he that planteth anything, neither he that watereth, but God that giveth the increase."[1] Take a grain of wheat and carefully examine it. In it is the germ which is to grow and bear the desired grain. In effecting this change from the seed to the harvest many agencies are necessary. There is the *soil.* God made that. There is the quality in the soil which may administer to the development and maturity of the grain. God made that. There are the early and the latter rains, and the light and heat of the sun, without which the change of the seed into the harvest cannot take place. God made these also. Besides these there is the *regulation* of the forces of nature. If the frost comes when the wheat is in blossom, or if the rain falls in too great abundance, or if it come not at all, or if the sun glare too fiercely on the unmoistened soil, or if it be enveloped too constantly in mists and fogs—the hopes of harvest must be disappointed.

[1] 1 Cor. iii. 6, 7.

The regulation of the seasons is a work which God alone can manage. From the agencies which are necessary to the development of seed-wheat into a harvest, subtract those which literally belong to God alone, and how little is left! Of the growth and maturity of all those plants and animals on which we live, God says to us, "Without me ye can do nothing."[1]

And yet, lest some might infer that he was teaching that God must do everything and man nothing, the apostle adds: "Now he that planteth and he that watereth are one, and *every man shall receive his* OWN REWARD *according to his* OWN LABOR."[2] As if the apostle had said: "As to the efficient power which converts the seed into the harvest, whether in the natural or moral world, *it* belongs to God alone. He alone gives the increase. But whilst this is true, God has so arranged his plans as to bless human effort so that every man shall receive his own reward according to his own labor."

If we would have a harvest, we must prepare the ground and sow the seed. This will not cause the seed to grow, and yet without this God will not cause it to grow. We must protect the

[1] John xv. 5. [2] 1 Cor. iii. 8.

field, and in due time gather the ripened grain. These acts of ours will not supplant the divine efficiency, and yet without these acts God will not give us overflowing granaries. In a few exceptional cases God as a sovereign has suspended this rule for a time, as when the ravens fed Elijah,[1] and when the widow's barrel of meal and cruse of oil did not waste,[2] and when the two miracles of Jesus were wrought, multiplying a very little food into an abundance, in the one case for four thousand people, and in the other for five thousand.[3]

This great principle prevails in the moral world. "Be not deceived: God is not mocked, for whatsoever a man soweth that shall he also reap. For he that soweth to his flesh shall of the flesh reap corruption, but he that soweth to the Spirit shall of the Spirit reap life everlasting."[4] "Work out your own salvation with fear and trembling, for it is God which worketh in you both to will and to do of his good pleasure."[5] It is objected that this latter exhortation is addressed to persons already regenerate. This is true,

[1] 1 Kings xvii. 6. [2] 1 Kings xvii. 14.
[3] Mark vi. 44; Matt. xv. 38. [4] Gal. vi. 7, 8.
[5] Phil ii. 12, 13.

but can it be more necessary for such a one to work out his own salvation than for one who is altogether in his sins?

"WHAT MUST I DO?"

There was a certain young man whose deportment was unexceptionable, whose integrity was above suspicion, and whose treatment of religion was deferential. Whatever may have been his private habits in regard to the reading of the Bible and prayer, he was a punctual attendant on Sabbath services and an attentive hearer of the gospel. Whilst he was very attentive to preaching, he rarely gave any signs of emotion as though he felt himself to be a sinner against God, in danger of eternal perdition. His pastor, having occasion to see him at his place of business, ventured to inquire whether he felt any concern about his future welfare. Without hesitation or impatience he replied that he had no anxiety, and that his mind was directed but little to the subject.

"You admit the necessity and importance of a change of heart in order to be saved, do you not?" asked his pastor.

"Certainly I do."

"And also that you have sinned greatly against

"What Must I Do?"

Page 180.

God in your heart, your words, your thoughts, your actions, and that you need God's forgiveness?"

"Oh yes, sir, certainly. I admit this."

"And that God can only forgive sin on account of the atonement which the Lord Jesus Christ hath made, and that in order to our receiving the benefits of this atonement we must believe in Christ?"

"I admit all this," he calmly and frankly replied.

"Why, then, do you not confess your sins to God, and ask him to forgive you for the sake of Christ?"

"Because I have no feeling which is deeper than a mere intellectual admission. I wish I did feel, but the fact is I do not."

"Suppose one of your customers who owes you should admit the justice of the claim and yet plead that he had no feeling about it. Would you think his plea sound?"

"No, of course not. He ought to pay the debt."

"Feeling or no feeling?"

"Of course he ought, for feeling has nothing to do with the matter."

"Your reasoning is just; why not apply it to the obligations you admit you owe to God? Why not set about this work, not because you *feel* like doing it, but because it is *right?*"

The young man was disturbed by those questions, but after a moment be said: "If you will tell me what to do, I will do it to the best of my ability!"

"There is an inquiry-meeting at my house to-night. Come, and by the coming show that you are an inquirer after the way of salvation. Will you?" asked his pastor.

"Yes."

He was faithful to his promise. He engaged in it as something to be accomplished. He read the Bible, he asked God for light, and he inquired of Christian people what he must do. It was not long before he had enough feeling about himself as a helpless, ruined and guilty sinner, and he was led to Christ apparently a true penitent. His inquiry was now for the will of God. "Lord, what wilt thou have me to do?" He would no longer live to himself, but unto Christ, who died for him. A new principle and motive of action had been implanted in his soul. Selfishness had given way to the love of God. He was a new creature in Christ; old things had passed away, behold, all things had become new.

Did he make himself a new creature? Had he been dead, he could as easily have raised himself to life. The Holy Spirit quickened him into life. And yet my young friend did a work which was necessary not as an efficient cause, but as a condition of salvation; he set himself earnestly to working out his salvation, inquiring after help, and obeying as fast as the light was imparted. God in spiritual as well as in less important matters "helps the man who helps himself;" in one who works out his own salvation with fear and trembling God worketh to do his own pleasure.

God gave my friend practical wisdom in the greatest of all concerns, *seeking his salvation,* and God gave him what he sought. Let us pray unto him to give us all this wisdom.

SOME SUGGESTIONS.

But you admit that the Holy Spirit of God is the author of this great change, and also that while God works in us to will and to do of his good pleasure, we must work out our own salvation with fear and trembling. Yet you ask,

"What must I do?" There are some suggestions which are worthy of a place here.

1. *Get clear views of your real character and danger.* Some people seem to think that God will miraculously impart to sinners a knowledge of certain facts already revealed and within their reach. Let me name a few as examples. God has told us that every descendant of Adam is a sinner; that in order to be saved a sinner must become a new creature in the new birth; that his heart must be so changed as to be constrained by the love of Christ, and not the love of self; that he must as a consequence and proof of this change live a holy life, bringing forth good works meet for repentance; and that if such a change be not wrought in the sinner's heart, he must perish for ever.

Here are certain facts made known for the express purpose of convincing sinners that they are the very persons whom Jesus came to call to repentance, the very ones who are sick and whom Jesus came to heal.

These facts are written with sunbeams in the Bible, which lies unopened and unread in very many dwellings. When Washington was crossing the Delaware, it is said that some Tory on the New Jersey side of the river sent a letter to

Colonel Rahl, the commander of the Hessians at Trenton, stating to him the fact. He was playing cards at the time, and thrust the letter unread into his pocket. It did him no more good than a piece of blank paper, simply because he neglected to read it. And would any one hint that the writer of that letter ought to have gone to Trenton to repeat information already in possession of the man? And will God by miracle reveal to sinners those great facts which are already taught them in his word?

Although elsewhere this thought has been stated, let me here repeat it, that the sinner who would be saved must diligently study God's word in order to get clear views of his real character and danger. Those who have narrowly watched religious awakenings have noticed that some persons are excited greatly and easily, but their feelings subside quickly, "because they had no deepness of earth." The shallowness and evanescence of their feelings might be traced to their ignorance and neglect of God's word. In many cases they are unacquainted with the most obvious facts and doctrines of that Book, and do nothing to repair the lack. They are usually inattentive hearers of preaching, take no pleasure in conversation with intelligent Christians, and none in the Sabbath-school and Bible-class instruction. The religious excitement of such is often hot as fires on the prairies, and as short lived. There is very little reliance to be placed in the exercises of a professed inquirer or convert who is ignorant of God's word, and who neglects to overcome that want by *searching the Scriptures.*

In scores of instances I have seen large numbers assembled to inquire what they must do. At first there would be very little marked difference in their exercises. All manifested more or less concern. In a short time some would profess conversion, and this would be a fact separating the inquirers into two classes. A part of those not converted invariably lost their feeling of anxiety. A careful inquiry into the habits of these short-lived inquirers showed that nine out of ten of them were habitual neglecters of the Bible. Of those who professed conversion, after a time some either went back or gave little evidence that they had experienced a change of heart. Here again the same fatal neglect may be found. The most of these who went back did not search the Scriptures. To such an extent is this true that I have no confidence in the soundness of an alleged conversion which may not be traced back to a knowledge of the Scriptures, or which is not fed and invigorated by communion with God in his Word.

The Bible teaches the sinner his real character by furnishing him a standard of judgment with which to compare his life and motives, and he never will have a clear knowledge of his own character and danger unless he either directly or indirectly derives it from this infallible source. To show how important this knowledge is to an inquirer after salvation let me use an illustration. A young man, a member of the Theological Seminary at Princeton, was unwell. There were symptoms of consumption, but he resolutely refused to look at them. He went to a milder climate, but found no permanent relief. His disease he persistently called a *throat* disease and not a disease of the *lungs*. At last, greatly prostrated, he called a physician of great skill, who told him that his lungs were diseased beyond all hope of relief, and that death was at the door. Then he was aroused and alarmed, and he hastened home to die, but not until he had exhausted the skill of the most skillful answering this question, "Cannot something be done to save my life?" The point is this: he showed no anxiety about a cure until he saw clearly that he was fatally sick. Had there been a physician able to cure him, he would not have gone to him for help so long as he did not believe that he needed help.

Let every inquirer study the Scriptures and his own heart to learn that this is his own character, "The heart is deceitful above all things and desperately wicked," and that this is his own personal danger, "The wicked shall be turned into hell." When these facts flame upon him he will look for help where help is to be obtained.

2. *Gain clear conceptions as to what help you need.* This must be determined by considering the circumstances and the word of God. If I am embarrassed with debt, the help I need will be of a pecuniary nature; hence it would be folly for me in such a case to appeal for help to a skillful physician who has little of "this world's goods."

If I am sick, the help I need is of a healing nature; hence it would be folly for me to appeal to some wealthy friend who has no medical skill. The services of the good physician would then be in place.

If I am threatened with personal violence by

some strong enemy, the help I need is not of a pecuniary or medical nature, but of a muscular sort that will shield me from my antagonist.

Your question, my inquiring friend, is this: "What must I do to be saved?" *What is the nature of this salvation?* You are condemned as a trangressor of the Law, hence you need help which shall remove this condemnation from your guilty soul. "How should man be just with God? If he will contend with him, he cannot answer him one of a thousand." This fact is asserted in various ways. Now our transgressions are represented as an immense debt which we cannot pay, and yet if we do not pay it we must be shut up in prison never to come out.[1] Then we need help to meet this fearful *debt.*

Now it is stated under the form of a sentence of death by the court. The sinner is condemned already:[2] "The soul that sinneth, it shall die."[3] The help you need, my friend, is of a kind that will take off this sentence and bring you forgiveness of sin.

Call it *debt* or *condemnation for capital crime,* you need assistance of a kind to meet your wants.

You have a very deceitful and desperately wicked

[1] Matt. xviii. 23-35. [2] John iii. 18. [3] Ezek. xviii. 20.

heart. Many people think this a statement not warranted by facts. Saul of Tarsus once thought very well of himself until the real wickedness of his heart was shown to him. Then he owned himself the chief of sinners.

This is a vital point, and any unsoundness here may be fatal; and here, it is to be feared, is the beginning of much unsatisfactory Christian experience. The insight of many awakened persons into their own hearts is so superficial that they hardly realize how wicked they are. They seem now to meditate profoundly on the tremendous words with which God describes the natural heart and sin—now to gaze long and intently into the depths of their own depraved hearts, until, alarmed and shocked, they are forced to cry out in despair, as did the apostle, "O wretched man that I am! Who shall deliver me from the body of this death?"

When you get a clear view of your own wicked heart, you will feel that you not only need forgiveness, but a *new creation.* "Ye must be born again."

Besides, your thoughts have worn deep channels in the wrong direction; you need help to force them into right channels. Your affections have been like the branches of a vine fallen to the earth and clinging to unworthy objects; you need help to raise them up to God, the only right Object of your supreme love. Your bodily powers have been the servants of sin, and you need help to subject them to God, a willing and living sacrifice.

And as you thus bring your thoughts to bear on your character and danger as a condemned sinner whose heart is desperately wicked, you will see that you need just such help as *Jesus* can give you, "for there is no condemnation to them which are in Christ Jesus,"[1] and such help as the Holy Spirit of God brings, for it is written that the sinner is saved "by the washing of regeneration and renewing of the Holy Ghost."[2]

In other words, these two suggestions simply bid you consider *what* you want and *who* is to supply it. You want to be saved, and that great salvation can only be brought you by the *Lord Jesus Christ*, the Saviour, and the *Holy Spirit* the Sanctifier.

3. *Pray for the help you need, and cast yourself on the divine mercy through Christ alone.* It is a very strange fact that there are persons who are

[1] Rom. viii. 1. [2] Tit. iii. 5.

unwilling and even ashamed to pray in secret. If poor, they will ask for help of their friends; if sick, they will ask help of the physician; if in distress, they will ask for help of those who are able to give it; but distressed with the fear of hell, a sense of guilt and condemnation, needing to be saved, and even wishing it, they will not ask for help of God, who only is able to help them. Many a proud heart revolts against bowing the suppliant knee to God, and especially to ask God to bestow on them undeserved mercy.

But the inquirer must pray for help. You have sinned against God, and you must ask God to forgive you for Christ's sake. You owe a great debt, and you must ask Christ to pay it for you. You lie under the sentence of death, and you must ask Christ to redeem you from the curse of the Law by taking your place.[1] You are dead in trespasses and sins[2]—that is, you are averse to holiness, you love sin, and to become a holy man transcends your power—and therefore you must pray the Holy Spirit to help your infirmities. You are wholly possessed with a wicked heart, and therefore you must pray, "Create in me a clean heart, O God, and renew a right spirit

[1] Gal. iii. 13; 2 Cor. v. 21. [2] Eph. ii. 1; Col. ii. 13.

within me." You are encompassed with difficulties, you are sinking under your sins, you are in the most extreme peril, and you must cry to your Saviour, as Peter did when he was beginning to sink in the waves, "Lord, save me."

You must pray, for Jesus says, "*Ask*, and it shall be given you; *seek*, and ye shall find; *knock*, and it shall be opened unto you. For every one that asketh receiveth; and he that seeketh findeth; and to him that knocketh it shall be opened."[1]

But you object that "the sacrifice of the wicked is an abomination to the Lord."[2] And so it is; and did you feel what you say, you would not cavil at this gracious privilege of prayer, nor would you wait until you cease being wicked before you pray, but you would do as the leper did when he knelt at the feet of Jesus, saying, "Lord, if thou wilt thou canst make me clean," and as the publican who said, "God be merciful to me a sinner."

You must ask very earnestly for the needed help.

And you must do more. *You must renounce all your own good works, and cast yourself on the mercy of God in Christ.* The farmer must pray

[1] Luke ii. 9, 10. [2] Prov. xv. 8.

for a blessing, but he must himself sow the seed which is to be blessed. The man with the withered hand must stretch it forth when commanded to do so. So you who are asking God to help you must also help yourself. You must renounce all trust in your own good works, and cease to go about to establish your own righteousness, which is of the Law.[1] You must cast yourself as a poor, ruined and helpless sinner on *Christ*, who "is the end of the law for righteousness to every one that believeth."[2] *You* must "confess with thy mouth the Lord Jesus, and believe in thine heart that God hath raised him from the dead"—in a word, *you* must believe in the Lord Jesus Christ in order to be saved.

You must pray for help, and yet you must help yourself with all your might, striving to enter in at the strait gate, and to work out your own salvation with fear and trembling, for it is God who worketh in you to will and to do of his good pleasure.[3]

[1] Rom. ix. 3. [2] Rom. x 4.
[3] Luke xiii. 24; Phil. ii. 12, 13.

CHAPTER XIII.

SIGNS OF THE CHANGE.

"BUT," you say, "if this change is one of such importance and necessity, it is very desirable to guard against mistakes. *How can I know that this change has taken place in me?*"

To see how vital a question this is we have only to refer to a class of facts which have transpired in every church. Persons there are who have for a time exhibited unusual religious zeal. They stood foremost in the ranks of pious people, and were ready to make any sacrifices for Christ. Very commonly such were not a little self-complacent in regard to what they esteemed their own superior piety, and even censorious in regard to their less zealous brethren. And yet how many such have gone back to "the beggarly elements of the world" and altogether ceased following Christ! They forsook the prayer-meeting, and even on the Sabbath rarely attended worship. It is charitable to say that such were mistaken in supposing themselves the subjects of this change of heart. There probably never was a circle of professed converts which did not have some of this class, nor a church which did not number some such members. Alas! of how many a professed convert it might be said, "He feedeth on ashes; a deceived heart hath turned him aside that he cannot deliver his soul nor say, *Is there not a lie in my right hand?*"

To aid you in avoiding such a mistake some signs may be named which show that "the heart has been changed," that it has been "born again."

These evidences may be arranged in two classes, INTERNAL and EXTERNAL.

INTERNAL EVIDENCES OF THE NEW BIRTH.

These are to be sought for in the convert's own spirit, and can only be inspected by himself and God.

DELIGHT IN GOD'S CHARACTER.

The truly regenerate soul is *more or less clearly conscious of delight in God's character.* This is a fundamental evidence, since the very essence of that depravity from which the sinner is converted is "enmity against God." Whenever the real feelings of the natural heart are developed, they are full of dislike of God's holy character, sovereignty, law and deeds. "Therefore they say unto God, Depart from us, for we desire not the knowledge of thy ways."[1] "But his citizens hated him and sent a message after him, saying, We will not have this man to reign over us."[2]

The light is good and pleasant to one whose eye is sound, but painful to the diseased eye. All holy beings love God because he is infinitely lovely, and as the soul is recovered from sin it also has this feeling toward God. The settled feeling of the truly "born again" is not enmity, but delight in God. "Whom have I in heaven," it cries, "but thee? And there is none upon the earth that I desire besides, or in comparison with thee."[3] When the apostle declares that such a one has "peace with God through our Lord Jesus Christ," he not merely means that God has removed the sentence of condemnation from the sinner, but that the sinner is "at one" with God in the sense that he admires and loves God. He looks at God as his Father in heaven.

[1] Job xxi. 14. [2] Luke xix. 14. [3] Ps. lxxiii. 25.

There may be a clearer consciousness of this delight in God at one time than at another, but it must be in the soul of one to be born again. It is not a selfish feeling, as if he were to say, "How happy I feel!" or "How good I am!" but "How lovely, how excellent, how holy, is God, whom I trust I now love!"

This is the feeling, the settled conviction of every converted soul, and he beholds God in his Word, his works, his providence and his gospel. He who professes conversion will be able to examine his own heart by this test: "Do I love God?" That conversion is spurious which is not marked by this necessary sign.

DESIRE TO DO GOD'S WILL.

But he will not only feel delight in God's character, *he will desire to fulfill God's will.*

Religion is not a mere ecstasy of feeling like that which one has as he sees the sun rise in the summer's morning, his beams shining through the deep green foliage and refracted into surpassing beauty through millions of dewdrops. One then exclaims, "How glorious the king of day! How unspeakably beautiful the morning!" This delight in the sun and the morning may be an evanescent emotion bearing no fruit. It is not so with the Christian's delight in God. It prompts him to desire to be a dutiful child. See that son who professes to admire and love his father. If he be sincere, he cannot sit still and gaze and admire, but he asks himself, "What can I do to show my love for my father?"

This rule is a very plain and discriminating one, which you may apply to your own alleged conversion. Turn your thoughts in upon your heart with this question: "Do I desire to do the will of God?" The question is not, Do you *do* that will *perfectly?* but, Do you *desire* to do it? That will of God often clashes with human inclination, and bids us do the things we would not and leave undone the things we would. The human heart has one rule, and God gives another which is very different, and we may be assured that when the love of God has uprooted the natural selfishness of the heart, love for God will beget the *desire to do the will of God.*

Take a case. A young man, having completed his studies at college, chooses to enter himself as a clerk in a bank. His diligence, integrity and capacity for business soon win for him promotion, until it is evident that it is "only a question of time" about his securing the highest position in that kind of business. All this while the love of self inspires him. God is not in all his thoughts. He is as really selfish as is the highway robber. But his mind was directed to this fact, and he saw that he was a *selfish, ungodly man.* He confessed his sin, and believed that he was forgiven. He trusted in Jesus Christ, and hoped he had been born again. What was one sign that he was not mistaken? This: he was not afraid to take his chosen, honorable and prided business before God, honestly to ask the question, "Lord, what wilt thou have me to do?" He meant by this question just this: "Lord, if it is thy will that I continue in this business, I will continue in it not to promote *my* interests, but to glorify thee. And if it is thy will that I leave this business in order to serve thee in another calling, I desire to do *that.*"

This is not a mere supposition. In its essential features it is a fact, and this convert left his lucrative employment to preach the gospel. By this it is not meant to utter the folly that every converted banker's clerk or lawyer or physician ought to leave that calling to preach the gospel. By no means. The Lord has need of good men in every honorable calling, but the young convert will not fail to notice the settling of the question of a calling in life, not by a desire to please himself, but to do the will of God. After a similar examination another man will as sincerely serve God as a banker.

This desire to fulfill the will of God is as essential to real piety as blood is to the living body.

EMPLOYMENTS APPROVED BY GOD.

The true Christian will *aim after employments and enjoyments which God approves.* Some years ago a young man, the son of an excellent minister in Connecticut, was settling himself in a Western town as a physician. He was a man of more than common gifts and force, and was well educated in his profession. His talents and energy soon made a favorable impression on the community, and he was likely to acquire a remunerative practice. In 1840 he "was converted soundly," and gave one proof of the fact by subjecting his favorite profession to this severe test, "Is this the employment God wishes me to follow?" He prayed over the matter with no little trouble of spirit, and weighed the claims of duty. It seemed to him that God called him to preach

Christ, but his wife and his friends thought otherwise. They said, "You are already successfully practicing medicine. A pious physician has many opportunities for usefulness. Your family need your support, and if you change your profession, for several years they must suffer. You ought to imitate the apostle who had learned in whatever state he was therewith to be content."

But this young man replied to all this excellent reasoning by the one answer: "It seems to me that God wishes me to make the change, and if so, I desire to do God's will at whatever sacrifice."

With great decision he began the change, and pursued his preparatory theological studies under very trying circumstances, but his faith and cheerfulness did not fail. He became the pastor of a Presbyterian church in Ohio, and was very successful in winning souls to Christ. He died in the prime of his manhood, and his weeping people buried him by the threshold of their new sanctuary. The monument which meets your eye as you enter the church is a mute witness to the assertion that one who is really converted will desire to choose the employment which pleases God.

Here is another fact. More than thirty years ago a certain country community was excited by the temperance reformation recently begun. The "Six Sermons on Intemperance," by Dr. Beecher, were read in the church on successive Sabbath afternoons. More than a hundred pledged themselves not to drink, or sell or furnish ardent spirits. Among these were several notorious drunkards. It was what is called "a *great apple year.*" The trees were loaded with apples, and thousands of bushels were taken to the distillery to be manufactured into rum on shares. One man, a professor of religion, owned extensive orchards, and had in his cellar a large amount of rum. His conscience was disturbed by the new light which revealed to him the evils of intemperance as he had never seen them before. The question was, "What is my duty? Ought I to join myself to this movement? But if I do, what about this rum I now have on hand, and these extensive orchards bearing fruit only fit for distilling purposes?"

If one might judge from his words and deeds, this man professing a change of heart did not ask whether it *would please God* if he should identify himself with the temperance reformation, but,

"*Can I afford the pecuniary loss which it will bring upon me?*" And what was this but a desire not to please God, but to save his money? The love of money was stronger than the love of God. And what did this prove? That he was not "born again," for no man is a Christian who loves son or daughter, lands or wife, more than God.[1] Five years after this time the man was awakened, and confessed himself an unconverted sinner. As such he was converted, and gave this sign of a heart-change, that he manifested a desire to do those things and enjoy those pleasures which God approves.

This is an unmistakable and necessary sign.

DESIRE TO BE PURE IN HEART.

But when one is born again he *loves and desires to be pure in heart.* All selfishness of heart is disagreeable to him, and all impurity of thought, affection or motive is a "body of death."[2] The Psalmist said, "I hate vain thoughts;"[3] "cleanse thou me from secret faults."[4] "Secret sins"[5] trouble him, and he is not content merely to be praised by his fellow-men as a good man, an ex-

[1] Matt. xix. 29; x. 37. [2] Rom. vii. 24.
[3] Ps. cix. 113. [4] Ps. xix. 12. [5] Ps. xc. 8.

emplary Christian, but he longs to be "pure in heart." A fair exterior is not enough. He prays for holiness of heart. No doubt Naaman was clothed in rich apparel, and for aught that we know his appearance was such as became so great a man, but "he was a leper." His reputation for bravery, his splendid position and garments, could not conceal from himself the loathsome disease which was the bane of his life. Others might admire his appearance and applaud his deeds, but he himself was compelled to think, "Woe is me, for I am a leper!"

The real Christian has a feeling akin to this as he looks at the imperfections which mingle in his motives, his thoughts and his spiritual exercises. It is not merely a question of reward and punishment, but, now that he has become "a new creature in Christ," he perceives that there is beauty in holiness, and that sin is "an evil thing and bitter." And hence he is inclined often to cry out earnestly, "Search me, O God, and know my heart; try me, and know my thoughts; and see if there be any wicked way in me, and lead me in the way everlasting."

Unconverted persons often notice the confession which Christians make of their great sins against God, and wonder whether they *are* such great sinners as they profess to be, or whether it is a mere affectation or habit. As compared with their fellow-men they are not great sinners, but as judged by the perfect holiness of God they feel themselves to be vile. In proportion as they advance in holiness does their perception of the hatefulness of sin grow keen.

A stranger was once admiring some beds of pinks. There were hundreds of flowers of every variety and color, and to him, with his ignorance of floral botany, they all seemed perfectly beautiful, but the gentleman who owned the garden remarked, "If I find a dozen *perfect* pinks among all these, I shall be satisfied." He then took one and said, "*You* think this perfect, but here is an imperfection which makes it look ugly to me." Why did the flower seem perfect to the one, but imperfect to the other? His knowledge of botany and his practical acquaintance with flowers accounted for the difference.

One may look at a work of art, a painting, a statue or a temple, and admire it, while a Michael Angelo or a Praxiteles, looking at the same work, would condemn it as defective in perspective, proportion, outline, color or some other quality.

What is no defect to one in his ignorance of art is a great blemish to the artist with his cultured eye.

It is thus with a real Christian. The nearer he draws to God, the clearer become his perceptions of the loveliness of holiness, the more hateful will sin appear to him. It is a notable fact that the Apostle Paul was not far from heaven when he exclaimed, "O wretched man that I am! Who shall deliver me from the body of this death?"[1]

LOVE FOR CHRIST.

One who is truly born again will not only believe in Christ for salvation, but *he will have a very tender love for Christ.* The answer of a professed Christian to the question, "What think ye of *Christ?*" involves an answer also to this question, "Am I a Christian?" It is true that "God so loved the world as to give his only begotten Son" to save it; it is also true that the Holy Spirit convicts, converts and sanctifies sinners. Yet the Lord Jesus Christ is the Mediator between God and man;[2] he came into the world to save sinners;[3] he was made sin for us,[4] and a curse for us, that he might redeem us from the curse

[1] Rom. vii. 24. [2] 1 Tim. ii. 5. [3] 1 Tim. i. 15. [4] 2 Cor. v. 21.

of the Law.[1] It was *Jesus* who humbled himself to become a child born of a woman made under the Law; it was *Jesus* who, being formed in fashion as a man, humbled himself and became obedient unto death—even the death of the cross. It was *Jesus* who suffered such agony in Gethsemane, such mockings and scornings in Pilate's judgment-hall, and such unspeakable anguish on Calvary. He did and suffered all this to save the sinner, and that sinner who professes to be born again, and yet has no love for Jesus his Saviour, *must* be mistaken. If he were truly converted, he would see Jesus with eyes clarified and heart quickened by gratitude. There was no extravagance in the expression of the apostle, "the love of Christ constraineth us,"[2] nor in that ever present tenderness which made it impossible for him to write or speak many words which did not include the name of Jesus.

A difference in natural temperament may modify the experiences of different Christians. One may be possessed of keen and excitable emotions; another may be dull and heavy, and not inclined to any outgush of feeling; another may have a placid temperament fitting him for quiet joy. This

[1] Gal. iii. 13. [2] 2 Cor. v. 14.

natural temperament will manifest itself in the love which each one shows for Christ. The first will often be dissolved in tearful tenderness, and his emotions will rush forth like a mountain brook. The second will be marked by a business-like air, a sluggish impassibility very much like a Western river. The third will not have the outgushing emotion of the first, nor sluggish emotions of the second, but his feelings are serene as a summer's sky, deep and clear as the waters of a Northern lake. But while there is this difference of manifestation, the thing manifested is the same in the three: it is the love of Christ. Ask each one the question, "Lovest thou Christ more than houses, or lands, or friends?" The first one may answer as impetuously and confidently as Peter, "Thou knowest that I love Christ." The second may answer you as he would a question in business, by simply saying, "Yes, I love Christ." The third may answer, with quiet serenity as different from the outburst of the first as summer's sunset is from a summer's shower,

> "How sweet the name of Jesus sounds
> In a believer's ear!"

One who is truly born again will love Christ.

How can it be otherwise with one who says, "I hope I am to be saved, because Jesus died to save me." Suppose a man on the sinking Arctic, without a life-preserver to bear him up, or a spar to cling to, or a boat to flee to. Death looks him in the face, and he sees no way to escape. But an entire stranger, on whose compassion he has no claims, takes his only life-preserver and gives it to him. By this act he is saved, but his benefactor is lost. Can he ever think of that benefactor without tender feeling? He may have more tenderness of feeling at one time than at another, but at all times there will be in his heart a fountain of affection for his benefactor as unfailing as a mountain spring.

LOVE FOR ALL MEN.

There is another internal evidence of this change—*the desire to love all men according to the will of God.* As has been repeatedly stated, love to God as a supreme affection is the source of all religion, and out of this flows love to our neighbor. The Apostle John affirms that "if a man say, I love God, and hateth his brother, he is a liar; for he that loveth not his brother, whom he hath seen, how can he love God, whom he hath not seen? And this commandment have we from him, That he who loveth God love his brother also."[1]

If we examine the petition, "Forgive us our debts as we forgive our debtors," and such commands as these, "Love your enemies; bless them that curse you; do good to them that hate you, and pray for them which despitefully use you and persecute you,"[2] we find that a real Christian must not only not hate any one, but he must in some important sense love every one, whatever his character or conduct.

The Scriptures divide the human family into two classes, the friends and enemies of God, the good and bad, the holy and wicked, saints and sinners. If one has been born again, he will wish well to all men, and pity the vilest and worst of men, and desire to do them good. He cannot habitually, intentionally and without sorrow indulge in ill-will, hatred or malignity against any one, it matters not how bad he is, nor how badly he has acted.

By this it is not implied that a real Christian is to approve a bad man or a bad action. He may condemn the sin and the sinner, and yet pray

[1] 1 John iv. 20, 21. [2] Matt. vi. 12; v. 44.

for the sinner's reformation and be grieved if he persists to his ruin.

LOVE FOR BELIEVERS.

But the one who is "born again" feels a *special* love to all who have experienced the same change and believe in the same Saviour. Thus the Apostle Peter says to Christians: "*Honor* (esteem) all men. LOVE the brotherhood."[1] The Apostle Paul says: "As we have therefore opportunity let us do good unto all men, especially unto them who are of the household of faith."[2] He calls them "no more strangers and foreigners, but fellow-citizens with the saints and of the household of God;"[3] therefore "be ye kind one to another, tender-hearted, forgiving one another, even as God for Christ's sake hath forgiven you."[4] Said our blessed Redeemer the night before he was to suffer: "This is my commandment, That ye love one another as I have loved you."[5] The Apostle John declares: "We know that we have passed from death unto life, because we love the brethren. He that loveth not his brother abideth in death."[6]

[1] 1 Peter ii. 17. [2] Gal. vi. 10. [3] Eph. ii. 19.
[4] Eph. iv. 32. [5] John xv. 12. [6] 1 John iii. 14.

It is a noticeable fact that persons who have passed through the same or similar trials have a peculiar attachment to one another. Thus, "the survivors of the Revolution," those who had together endured the hardship of settling in a new country, or those who had escaped the perils of a shipwreck, have a mutual sympathy on that account. All Christians have felt the sting of conviction, the crushing weight of condemnation and the joy of pardon through Jesus, and they are anticipating the blessedness of being at home where the wicked cease from troubling and where the weary be at rest.

It must be more than a mere *show* of politeness, an external courtesy of manner. In his heart as well as life the one who has passed from death to life will "love the brethren."

These are some of the internal evidences of a change of heart, and, honestly tried by these tests, how many a professed conversion would appear to be as worthless as "the hypocrite's hope, ... which shall be cut off, and whose trust shall be a spider's web!"[1]

[1] Job viii. 13, 14.

EXTERNAL EVIDENCES OF CONVERSION.

Leaving those evidences of a change of heart which come only under the inspection of one's self and God, we now examine some which are external, and of course open to the inspection of men.

Our blessed Redeemer in a single sentence has expressed the signs of a heart-change: "If ye LOVE ME, KEEP MY COMMANDMENTS;" "If a man love me, he will keep my words."[1] To love Christ supremely is to be a new creature. That love is a spiritual principle in the heart, hidden from the view of man. But an outward obedience to Christ's words as the result of that hidden love is a fact which is open to human inspection.

DOING THE WILL OF GOD.

Hence it is an obvious remark that one who has experienced this change of heart *will strive to do the will of God.* He may not do that will perfectly, but he will *try* to do it. Whenever or wherever he finds the will of God he will aim to do it, or if he fails to do so, that delinquency will fill him with sorrow. For instance, God says: "Remember the Sabbath day to keep it holy."[2]

[1] John xiv. 15–23. [2] Ex. xx. 8.

A converted man will try to observe this rule. He may lift a sheep out of the pit on the Sabbath, and he may "loose his ox or his ass from the stall and lead him away to watering,"[1] or do any other act of *mercy* or *necessity*, but he will not travel on the Sabbath merely for business or pleasure or convenience. He will not plough or sow or reap or gather into barns, or engage in the labor of a secular calling or in worldly pleasures on that day.

God commands us to "do that which is honest,"[2] to put away lying and speak every man truth with his neighbor,[3] "to live soberly, righteously and godly in this present world,"[4] and to let our light so shine before men that they may see our good works and glorify our Father which is in heaven.[5] The man who is dishonest in his dealings, lying in his words and wicked in his actions, not occasionally under the power of sudden temptation, but intentionally, persistently and without sorrow before God, is not a Christian; he has not been born again. The rule is perfectly plain and it is as unchangeable as God: "If ye love me, keep my commandments."

[1] Matt. xii. 11; Luke xiii. 15. [2] 2 Cor. xiii. 7.
[3] Eph. iv. 25. [4] Tit. ii. 12. [5] Matt. v. 16.

On Patmos, amid visions of surpassing glory, the glorified Son of God said: "*Blessed are they that do his commandments.*"[1] And repeating the same sentiment John said: "He that keepeth his commandments dwelleth in him and he in him."[2]

A real Christian will not *as a habit* see how nearly he can approach the line which divides a good action from a bad one, a holy life from a wicked one. A higher rule controls him, and it is this: "Abstain from all appearance of evil."[3] We all know how easy it is to incur moral guilt, and yet to escape the censure of human laws. Suppose a man pays his creditor a certain sum of money, alleging it to be what he owes him. The creditor does not count the money, and will therefore never know that a part of the money due was not paid. His debtor detects his own mistake, and is sure that his creditor is not aware of it. If he be a good man, he will repair that mistake as readily as if there were a thousand witnesses to the transaction.

Or suppose that he has intentionally and cruelly wronged one who was in his power. He did it

[1] Rev. xxii. 14. [2] 1 John iii. 24.
[3] 1 Thess. v. 22.

before his conversion, but now that the love of God is the supreme motive of his inner life, he will be ready to imitate Zaccheus and say, "If I have taken anything from any man by false accusation, I restore him fourfold."

In a word, such a man in all the transactions of life will try to do right not because others see him, and the opposite course would injure his reputation, but because he is seeking to do the commandments of God.

There is a style of life which is called Christian, but which is not Christian. It consists in a sort of gravity of demeanor and a round of observances. It has a time for prayer and for worship. It surveys its duties into regular and square proprieties. Its observances are too refined and spiritual for the common deeds of life. When "the programme" of religious proprieties has been complied with, the man is ready to call it "*done,*" and to descend to a lower sphere in which the religious element is not to enter. As a worshiper of God he was devout and punctilious, but religion must keep itself within its own bounds, and not defile its garments by mixing with common men in common every-day life! This is no caricature. "O my soul, come not thou into their secret; unto their assembly, mine honor, be not thou united."

Not for the purpose of cavil at religious people as is the custom of some, but to show the necessity of bringing our religion into all our dealings, the remark of a gentleman who was skeptical may be repeated: "You talk of religion as a controlling force, changing the heart and purifying the life. My brother —— is a Quaker. How beautiful his life! How simple-hearted his integrity! How admirable his kindness! I can understand his life, and it commands my approbation. But come with me into the church whose doctrines you are offering to my acceptance. Look down that broad aisle, and select a few men who profess to be living under the control of religious principle. There is Mr. A., wholly absorbed in the acquisition of money. I tell you, if his life be a sign, Mammon and not God governs Mr. A. There is Mr. B., who does not hesitate to take the advantage of a man's embarrassments to help himself. With vast sums at his command, he has no compassion on those unfortunate enough to be in his power. There is Mr. C., in some respects the best lawyer in the city, but he is as cruel as the grave and as relentless as death. Yet you say the essence of religion is love to God and love to man!"

And in this strain he commented on individual characters, giving me, as he said, "Such a view as one took of them in business and actual life. They look well enough on the Sabbath and in church, but in their dealings every day they are apparently no better than men of no religious pretensions!"

He had selected the worst specimens from that church, and where there were five or ten against whom such charges would be true, there were at least fifty times as many against whom no such charges could be maintained. Yet those few illustrate the view here presented, that if the heart has experienced a change, that change will show itself not merely in the proprieties of religious worship, but in the business and pleasures of common life. Meet such a man "on 'change," in the counting-room, in the law-office, in the court-room, as debtor, creditor, counselor, or judge, in trifling and in great transactions, or meet him in the shop or at the loom or plough, and you say, "He is a good man, and the kind of religion which governs him is what the world wants and will be the better for having!"

"By their fruits shall ye know them," and it is only needful to repeat once more the all-comprehensive sign given by our Lord: "If a man love me, he will keep my word." Thousands who have very little knowledge of theology, and make no pretensions to learning or wit, are able to detect this sign of a change of heart, that he who has experienced it is trying to keep God's commandments and to glorify God by doing right in all situations.

SELF-DENIAL.

There is another external sign of conversion which deserves separate mention—*self-denial for the sake of Christ.* "If any man will come after me, let him deny himself, and take up his cross and follow me."[1] Human nature gravitates strongly toward self-indulgence, and a real convert will resist this tendency. It may be easier to abstain from warning a sinner to flee to Christ than to be faithful, but he will deny his selfish inclinations this indulgence. It may gratify his pride of position to indulge either in expensive adornments of person or home, so as to interfere with the urgent calls for help to preach the gospel to

[1] Matt. xvi. 24.

every creature. If so, he will deny himself in this respect for Christ. And thus by the duties and labors he performs, and the self-indulgences from which he refrains, he shows that he is denying himself for Christ.

As things exist in this world there can be no genuine change of heart which will not show itself in self-denial for Christ. This is evident from such declarations as these: "Whosoever doth not bear his cross and come after me cannot be my disciple."[1] "Yea, all that will live godly in Christ Jesus shall suffer persecution."[2] "Strive to enter in at the strait gate."[3] The same fact is implied in another class of declarations: "It is good neither to eat flesh nor to drink wine, nor anything whereby thy brother stumbleth, or is offended, or is made weak."[4] "If ye live after the flesh, ye shall die; but if ye through the Spirit do mortify the deeds of the body, ye shall live."[5]

The drift of these declarations cannot be mistaken, and if a person professes to be converted, and yet feels no strong purpose to check and put down his own selfish inclinations, doing many a duty which was painful and trying and leaving

[1] Luke xiv. 27. [2] 2 Tim. iii. 12. [3] Luke xiii. 24.
[4] Rom. xiv. 21. [5] Rom. viii. 13.

untouched many an indulgence greatly desired, he ought to doubt his own piety and re-examine the grounds of his hope.

A PUBLIC PROFESSION.

One truly born again *will identify himself with God's people by a public profession of Christ unless prevented by some extraordinary reason.* Even in the times when a public profession of Christ could not be made without the risk of property, social position and life, the Christian must avow his faith in Christ. This is evident from such a declaration as this, "Whosoever doth not bear his cross and come after me cannot be my disciple."[1] The manner in which Nicodemus and Joseph of Arimathea are mentioned marks with condemnation the attempt to be a disciple of Christ secretly.[2] The Apostle Paul earnestly enforces the same duty: "Wherefore come out from among them, and be ye separate, saith the Lord.[3]

This is one duty which our blessed Lord commands every disciple to perform—*to commemorate his death by the communion of the Lord's Supper:* "This do in remembrance of me." I see no dis-

[1] Luke xiv. 27. [2] John iii. 2; xix. 38. [3] 2 Cor. vi. 17.

cretion in this matter. A disciple of Christ is solemnly bound to do this, if it be possible for him to do it. He must not aim to be a disciple secretly, performing religious duties in secret, whilst in the world he is regarded as opposed to Christ. He must say to the world, "I am the Lord's, ... and subscribe with his hand unto the Lord, and surname himself by the name of Israel."[1] As soon as he hopes he is born again he must desire not to be secretly a follower of Jesus but apparently a servant of the devil, but to be altogether on the Lord's side.

No doubt many make a fatal mistake in this respect, and get into the Church without conversion. Through neglect to examine themselves they were deceived. This does not contradict the assertion that the desire to profess Christ before men is one sign of the new birth.

PEACE IN GOD.

Finally, a true convert will *have peace in God as an evidence that he has passed from death to life.*

There may be danger of putting undue stress on this point and making it a stumbling-block in

[1] Isa. xliv. 5.

the way of drooping Christians. The general truth that one who is "born again" ought to rejoice is evident in such sayings as these. Thus Jesus said, "Peace I leave with you, my peace I give unto you, not as the world giveth give I unto you. Let not your heart be troubled, neither let it be afraid."[1] Even to those who are persecuted, Jesus says, "Rejoice in that day and leap for joy: for, behold, your reward is great in heaven."[2] Repeatedly the Apostle Paul commands his brethren to "rejoice in the Lord," as if it were not merely a privilege, but a necessary sign of the new birth.

There are times in the experience of real Christians when the soul is filled with gloom, sorrow and despondency, but this is not the prevailing feeling. One who has been justified by faith in Jesus has peace with God,[3] one who has passed from death unto life must feel joy in pardon, and one who both desires and expects to reach heaven not merely has the right to rejoice and to be exceeding glad, but it is his duty thus to rejoice.

[1] John xiv. 27. [2] Luke vi. 23. [3] Rom. v. 1.

Labor the Road to Vigor.

Page 225.

CHAPTER XIV.

CHILDHOOD AND MANHOOD.

LET us suppose two boys of equal health and robustness to pursue the one an effeminate, the other a manly, course of life. The first one indulges in a luxurious and indolent style of living; the other lives on plain but nutritious diet, and engages in manly labor and pleasures. The one daintily avoids all unnecessary exertion, except perhaps in an over-heated ball-room; the other disdains not to hold the plough, to swing the axe or wield the spade. The first is famous at reclining on the luxurious sofa or composing himself to quietness in the rocking-chair; the other delights in riding the horse and in climbing the mountains.

A few years pass away, and the two boys have become men. They began with equal health and vigor, but how is it now? The one who has pursued the effeminate course of life is not the equal of the other, whose hard muscles, well-developed chest and limbs, ruddy complexion, elastic step and tough endurance prove the adaptation of his manly course of life to the development of a manly man. The main difference between the two is to be found in their ways of living. You cannot develop a vigorous manhood by stuffing a boy with confectionery and deforming him in a rocking-chair. Proper food, raiment and exercise are essential to the rounding out of a child into a "perfect man."

The development of the religious life in a converted soul has been compared to the growth of the body. The Apostle Paul calls the Christian who has been rightly trained a perfect man, who may come "unto the measure of the stature of the fullness of Christ."[1] He exhorts those who have been truly born again to "be no more children tossed to and fro.[2] "Brethren, be not *children* in understanding; howbeit in malice be ye children, but in understanding be *men*."[3]

These direct assertions are made more impressive by such figures as the apostle derives from the athletic games of his day: "So run that ye

[1] Eph. iv. 13. [2] Eph. iv. 14. [3] 1 Cor. xiv. 20.

may obtain. . . . . I therefore so run, not as uncertainly; so fight I not as one who beateth the air." "Let us run with patience the race set before us." "I have fought a good fight, I have finished my course." These figures point to a well-developed and vigorous Christian manhood, which is in strong contrast with the weakness of childhood and a manhood for some cause ill-formed and without vigor.

Suppose a young man who has just been converted should ask what course to pursue in order to become "a perfect man," one who in a spiritual sense will be fitted to fight, to wrestle, to run? He desires not merely to live, but to be strong and active, a spiritual athlete, and not a mere babe or imbecile.

In order to apprehend the force of the question let us consider two facts. Two young men, both of whom gave proof of a change of heart, became members of one church. The one for many years has remained about in the same place spiritually. He attends church regularly and partakes of the communion. He is in "good and regular standing," and no one can say aught against him, and yet he has not grown as a Christian. He is like a dwarf, whom time and food are unable to enlarge or strengthen. No one thinks of him as "a growing Christian."

The other young man when he was received into the church seemed in most respects on terms of equality with the first. He then gave no better evidences of a change, and was not regarded as the more promising of the two. As time moved on it became evident that he was "a growing man." There was a tone to his prayers and a ring in his exhortations which, associated with a very consistent life, won for him great consideration. It was known that he would be at the conference and prayer-meeting unless prevented by a good reason, and his brethren felt refreshed by his presence. He was not there merely to "count one," but as a living man he was there to get and to impart religious influence. It is so in every sphere in which he moves. He is not what he was twenty-seven years ago, and the difference is just this, then he was a *child*, but now he is a *man*.

It may well be said that these young converts then were children, but since then the one has advanced but little beyond the original starting-point, "for he is a babe,"[1] whilst the other has grown into a vigorous Christian man.

[1] Heb. v. 13.

Wherefore this difference so marked? How can a young convert gradually cast off the swaddling-clothes of childhood and attain this manhood? To the question let an answer be given as simple and practical as possible, appealing to the word of God and the experiences of Christian people as my authority.

There are two suggestions which will include the answer. They relate to the inner and the outer life as they bear on Christian manhood.

THE INNER LIFE AND CHRISTIAN MANHOOD.

Every Christian has what may be called an *inner* and an *outer* life. They both have important relations to a well-developed Christian manhood. Look at that Greek boy in his native village, engaged in rugged sports and conflicts. He has seen *men* running or wrestling or boxing or hurling the discus, and perhaps he has seen the far-famed Olympian or Isthmian games. In his heart is the settled purpose to fit himself to contend for the mastery in these contests. That purpose is the beginning of an inner life to him. As he grows up he meditates on the difficulties and glories of the conflict; he studies the history of particular heroes who have won the prizes; he practices temperance in meats and drinks; he hardens his muscles and toughens his sinews by manly exercises. In a word, in seclusion he is fitting himself for action in more conspicuous positions. When at last he enters the amphitheatre and wins the prize, he acts out the purposes and the training of his inner life.

It is so with the Christian man. He has a life of meditation and a life of action which are in such relations that neither is complete without the other. The Christian athlete must look to both the life within and the life without if he would attain unto "the measure of the stature of a perfect man."

SELF-KNOWLEDGE.

In considering the relation of the inner life to Christian manhood, we may notice that it involves *self-knowledge.* Many of the mistakes of men would have been avoided had they known themselves, and in this self-acquaintance is one secret source of success with many men. Owing to a lazy unwillingness to take the gauge of their faculties, or to a life of active restlessness, many men fail to select the sphere in life for which they are fitted. In order to growth and right development a Christian must know himself. He may be hot-tempered, or he may be indolent, or he may be covetous, or he may be jealous, or he may be envious, or he may be censorious, or he may be morally weak in some other characteristic or habit. It is his "weight," his "easily-besetting sin," which he must lay aside in order to run the Christian race. It is the weakness which his enemy is likely to find out to his injury. Self-knowledge will teach him to fortify himself at any such point. This is of the more importance, as it is a singular fact that a person is very much inclined to consider himself entirely secure at the very point of weakness.

Every one has a sphere in which he can do more good than in any other, and it is his duty to try to find it. Perhaps he ought to preach, or to teach, or to sell and buy, or to plough, or to plane. To find that right position he must know himself, or he will be likely to preach when he ought to plough, or to be ploughing when he ought to be preaching. This self-knowledge, pertaining to the inner life of the Christian, is of great importance. For want of this some men have made irreparable mistakes. David, cumbered with Saul's armor, was not so embarrassed as many a Christian has been when he has worked himself out of his proper place.

THOUGHT ON THE WORK TO BE DONE.

This inner Christian life also includes *careful meditation on the attainment to be made and the work to be done.* As a general rule, it will be found that success in all difficult undertakings has been preceded by an earnest study of the thing to be done. Thus Whitney brooded over the need of a machine to separate the seed from the fibre of the cotton, and the immense advantages of such an invention. Hence the cotton-gin, which has added thousands of millions of dollars to human wealth. So also Fulton and Stephenson; the one pondered on the advantages of applying steam to the driving of boats, the other of driving land-carriages. Hence we have the steamer and the locomotive.

The Christian must meditate on what God requires him *to be* and *to do.* He is to be holy; let him meditate on that requirement until he begins to realize its meaning in the character and the law of God. He is to do the commandments of God under the controlling power of supreme love to God, and he must also strive to obey those commandments perfectly in thought, word and deed; let him meditate until his whole soul is agitated with a view of what God requires him *to be* and *to do*. He will be like the Greek athlete who has witnessed the games and studied the thews and forces of his competitors, until he feels that, in order to victory, his own thews and forces must be developed into positive superiority over theirs. But for this he may be careless and unaspiring, and in consequence fail.

For want of this habit many Christians fail to grow in grace, make little advancement in holiness and duty.

HELPS AND HINDRANCES.

But this inner Christian life also includes an intelligent examination of what may be called *helps* and *hindrances*. If an engineer were to draft the plan of a tunnel through a mountain, he would not content himself until he had determined the nature of the helps and hindrances. The first question would relate to the desirableness of the tunnel, the next to the money at command for boring it, and the next to hindrances. He strikes the balance and says, "It can be done," or "It cannot be done." In all human enterprises the helps and the hindrances are carefully weighed, and it should be so with the Christian.

What are his helps to be and to do what God requires? Let him consider that "God is the strength of my heart,"[1] that "God is our refuge and strength, a very present help in trouble,"[2] and that "likewise the Spirit also helpeth our infirmities,"[3] and then he may say, "I can do all things through Christ which strengtheneth me,"[4] "The Lord is the strength of my life; of whom shall I be afraid?"[5]

Is this help *accessible?* Yes, for it is written, "Ask, and it shall be given you;"[6] indeed, so greatly does God wish his people to ask him for help that he says, "Before they call I will answer; and while they are yet speaking I will hear."[7]

The traveler from home often carries with him "bills of credit," enabling him wherever he is to draw money for his wants. The Christian has this help in the form of exceeding great and precious promises, and he ought to be fully persuaded that what God has promised he is able also to perform. If he would impart force to his

[1] Ps. lxxiii. 26. [2] Ps. xlvi. 1. [3] Rom. viii. 26.
[4] Phil. iv. 13. [5] Ps. xxvii. 1. [6] Matt. vii. 7.
[7] Isa. lxv 24.

inner life, let the Christian often take down the book of "drafts, payable on sight," which God has put in his hands. It would be a miracle to have a vigorous inner and outer Christian life without feeding both upon "the sincere milk of the word" and also its "strong meat."

But he has *hindrances* as well as helps, and he will consider them also. His own unsanctified nature, evil habits and companionships, "the world, the flesh and the devil," all pass in review, so that he is not surprised by them as if they were new enemies. He does not vauntingly say, "And now shall mine head be lifted up above mine enemies round about me,"[1] until he has considered who and how strong those enemies are.

THE REWARD.

The inner Christian life is also nourished by meditations on the *reward that will be given to him that is faithful.* It is true that in a sense "we are unprofitable servants," even when we have done our duty, and that in the sense of *merit* no one can hope for a reward. All is of grace, and yet that grace moves Jesus to say to some, "Well done, good and faithful servants," and lays the

[1] Ps. xxvii. 6.

ground for expecting that the Lord, the righteous Judge, will give a crown of righteousness unto that faithful servant. The Greek wrestler often thought of the crown which the victor won, the applause of the spectators and the welcome home, scarcely less honorable than the crown itself.

It is not merely a privilege, but it is a duty, for the Christian to nourish his spiritual strength by meditating on the reward that shall be bestowed on him at the last day. In the light of Moses as condensed by the apostle are two sentences which lay bare the secret impulses of his soul: "he had respect unto the recompense of the reward," and "he endured as seeing Him who is invisible."[1] We have seen that every Christian has real difficulties in his way, and if he would encourage his heart, renew his strength and vanquish his difficulties, let him meditate much on heaven as the home and reward of Christ's disciple. How many a sigh is stifled, how many a grief assuaged, how many a conflict successfully terminated, how many a temptation silenced, how many a fire quenched, by so meditating on heaven as contrasted with earth, the New Jerusalem with

[1] Heb. ii. 26, 27.

this earthly house of our tabernacle, that the Christian can say in transport,

> "O my sweet home, Jerusalem,
> Thy joys when shall I see?
>
> "Our sweetness mixed is with gall,
> Our pleasures are but pain,
> Our joys not worth the looking on,
> Our sorrows aye remain.
> But *there* they live in such delight,
> Such pleasure and such play,
> That unto them a thousand years
> Seems but as yesterday.
>
> "Jerusalem! Jerusalem!
> Thy joys fain would I see;
> Come quickly, Lord, and end my grief,
> And take me home to thee!"

THE EXAMPLE OF SAINTS.

The inner Christian life may be also invigorated by meditating on the *examples of those who have entered into rest.* This is the very idea on which the apostle builds the eleventh chapter of his epistle to the Hebrews. The hero-saints of past ages were summoned from the grave to become the models of those who were yet on earth. Abel, and Enoch, and Noah, and Abraham, and Moses, and others like them, are named for the study of

Christians. They were not angels, but men, who attained such a spiritual manhood in the face of as serious difficulties as oppose us to-day.

"Once they were mourning here below,
And wet their couch with tears;
They wrestled hard, as we do now,
With sins and doubts and fears."

It is a fact stated in the lives of persons distinguished in some calling that they have had some model before them to mould their characters and inspire their actions. The power of this intimate communion with a model character is wonderful. What an influence the characters drawn by Homer have had on the warriors of all succeeding ages! How some men have by intense meditation on the manners and deeds of Alexander, Cæsar and Napoleon seemed to reproduce those characters in their own souls and lives! How powerful the influence of John Howard and Florence Nightingale on those whose minds have gone out to commune with them in their deeds of Christ-like goodness! It is almost needless to add that the same principle perverted is the great corrupter of thousands who ponder, admire and imitate the foul heroes of the pirate ship, the robber's den and the ruffian's ring. It is this which constitutes the web and woof of the apostle's emphatic warning, "Be not deceived; evil communications corrupt good manners."[1] To be in constant contact and communion with a character which is bad or good in a marked degree is to undergo an assimilation to that character—at least, such is the tendency. "He that walketh with wise men shall be wise; but a companion of fools shall be destroyed."

Hence, the Christian may nourish his spiritual life by meditating often and earnestly on those great characters who once ran this race and fought this good fight, and won this crown of righteousness. The company of an earnest Christian is a hopeful blessing, and the memory of a saint tends to elevate us above the earthly. Who can meditate on the names of Moses, Joseph and Paul without becoming a better and more zealous Christian? If one shuts himself up in some narrow fissure in society into which no earnest working Christian comes, and in which the memory of no saint like a brilliant star sheds light, he will be narrow and one-sided in his views and weak and simple in his inner life. He may be a real

[1] 1 Cor. xv. 33.

Christian, but it is in the sense in which a fool or an idiot is a man.

COMMUNION WITH GOD.

Finally, the inner Christian life is made strong by *communion with God.* Much that has been said in the previous remarks is applicable here. God is the supreme centre and governor of the Christian's soul, and his love is the mainspring of all his actions. Hence, if one has been truly converted—that is, if the supreme selfishness of his heart has been succeeded by supreme love to God—he must of necessity think much of God. So the Psalmist: "My meditation of him shall be sweet. I will be glad in the Lord." "My soul waiteth for the Lord more than they that watch for the morning."[1]

An affectionate son was very sick, and in proportion to his weakness did his thoughts and affections go out toward his mother. If she were in the room, he loved to look at her, to hear her voice and to feel her hand. No one was able so well as she to smooth his pillow, arrange his food and medicine and administer those almost nameless delicacies of word, look and deed which

[1] Ps. civ. 34; cxxx. 6.

cheer up an invalid's chamber like the light of the morning. If she were absent even for a little while, he was thinking of her and wishing for her return. With such an affection for his mother and at such a season of weakness not many moments could pass without his thoughts dwelling upon her, and the more his thoughts dwelt upon her character and maternal goodness, the stronger grew his affection for her.

It is even so with the Christian. He loves God, and God is in his thoughts. There are seasons when he experiences that joy which arises from a sense of God's special presence in his soul. This inward experience he finds especially when he meditates upon God as infinite, holy, good, and as manifest in the person of Christ. He looks at God as infinitely glorious and lovely; and as one is refreshed by looking at the person and thinking of the character of some dear and noble friends, so is the Christian in thinking of God, only in an infinitely higher degree.

He also invigorates his inner life by reading of God in the Holy Scriptures. "The heavens declare the glory of God and the firmament showeth his handiwork," but the statutes and the word of the Lord are perfect, pure, clean, enduring for ever, and more to be desired than gold,[1] because they describe God to the Christian. As with anointed eyes he reads this word he experiences the benediction of Christ: "Blessed are the pure in heart, for they shall see God." The error of the natural heart esteeming God to be altogether such a one as itself is corrected by meditating on God as he is revealed in his word.[2] He who would have a vigorous life in his soul must come near to God by thinking much on his word.

But by PRAYER the Christian in a special sense communes with God. The great Teacher says to him: "When thou prayest enter into thy closet, and when thou hast shut thy door pray to thy Father which is in secret, and thy Father which seeth in secret shall reward thee openly."[3] If a gardener should at night enrich and moisten the soil about a vine, his secret labor would bring him a reward open to the inspection of all in the thriftiness of its growth and the abundance of its fruit. The culture was in secret, but the fruit was not in secret.

Thus also a Greek athlete might spend years of the most patient preparation for the national games. Very temperate in his food, very regular

[1] Ps. xix. 1–11. [2] Ps. l. 21. [3] Matt. vi. 6.

in sleep, and very zealous and indefatigable in his development of every physical force, yet his preparation would be in secret. It would be carried on in retirement, known only to a few, but when he steps into the arena his muscular and agile body and his victory in each toughly-contested conflict would be his open reward. The latter would be the legitimate result of the former.

It is so with the Christian man. If in secret he commune with his heavenly Father by supplication, thanksgiving and adoration, if in his closet he tell God his wants and his sins, his weaknesses and his sorrows, and in that sacred retirement wrestle with God as Jacob did, saying, "I will not let thee go except thou bless me," then shall he be so "filled with all the fullness of God," so shall God's strength be made perfect in his weakness, that he may in truth be called "ISRAEL," a prince of God, for as a prince he has "power with God and with men."[1]

There was a certain humble Christian woman moving in a humble and retired sphere. She was the youngest child of a large family, and from her earliest infancy was afflicted with such infirmities of body as often put her life in jeo-

[1] Gen. xxxii. 26–28; Eph. iii. 19; 2 Cor. xii. 9.

pardy and constantly shaded it with pain. This delicacy of health inclined her friends to the amiable fault of too much indulgence. They did not think she would be with them long, and they unwisely refrained from laying unwelcome restraints upon her inclinations. As she grew up to womanhood, she became more and more peevish and fretful. Ill-health and ill-training had combined to make her wretched, and also those about her. Naturally very benevolent and tender-hearted, she distressed her friends with her jealousy of being overlooked or undervalued. In natural gifts she possessed only ordinary talents, and these had received no very careful culture in early life.

That woman was converted to God, and it is not a rash assertion that without doubt now in heaven she is shining "as the brightness of the firmament" and "as the stars for ever and ever," because she was wise to "turn many to righteousness." Rarely was there a more devout Christian in the sphere she occupied. She was one whose piety was above suspicion. In the Sabbath-school her success was very remarkable. It was a rare occurrrence that a youth could be in her class a number of months without manifesting anxiety about his soul's salvation. In the midst of surrounding coldness there was a perennial revival in her class, like the verdure about a fountain in the desert. The most of her scholars were converted, and gave good evidences of piety. People wondered at the results, but could those who wondered have looked into the humble dwelling which she occupied they would have seen two facts —not casual but constant facts—which explained her success in winning souls to Christ. Lying open on the bed was her well-worn Bible, which she diligently perused when she was resting herself. She did not merely read it, but laboriously committed portions of it to memory so that she seemed to speak in the language of that Book even about the common transactions of life. This sacred word was the light to her feet, and it was also the food to her soul. But this was only one secret of her success, for by that bed was a chair at which she knelt before God in holy communion and faith at least as often as the Psalmist, who says: "Seven times a day do I praise thee because of thy righteous judgments." Because she searched the Scriptures and invigorated her inner life by communion with God, in spite of serious obstacles she lived most happily and successfully, and died in the full assurance of hope.

The lines of thought here discussed concerning the inner Christian life are of very great importance, and are in conflict with the tendencies of Christian experience in our times. There is far too little attention paid to this inner life as the source of a vigorous and well-proportioned outer life. The great saints of the old dispensation, and of the new also, were men who meditated profoundly, read the Holy Scriptures reverently, wrestled in prayer as for their lives, and who travailed in birth until Christ was formed in their souls, and we shall not vie with them in their excellence and triumphs until we imitate them in their attention to the inner life of the soul, keeping with all diligence the heart, out of which are the issues of life.

THE OUTER LIFE AND CHRISTIAN MANHOOD.

A LIFE OF ACTIVE DUTY.

A life of active duty is necessary to the development of a Christian manhood. One may hide himself in a monk's cell a score of years, kneeling before a picture or a cross, meditating on the passion of Christ and the love of God, and yet he will not attain that which we choose to name "Christian manhood." Nor will he attain it by living a life of meditation in any seclusion whatever, reading the choicest religious books, including the Bible, praying fervently and singing devoutly. He would become a "perfect man" by such a course no sooner than a young Greek could become a triumphant athlete by meditating on the heroes of the games without an effort to imitate their actions. He may become posted in the theory and facts of religion, he may be a sound theologian, and yet he will be a one-sided man, an imperfect man, and not one who has come "unto the measure of the stature of the fullness of Christ." If a man should follow some occupation which should develop the arms and chest, but shrivel the rest of his body, or which should enlarge and intensify his brain, draining away the blood and vital forces of the body to this one organ, the development could be no more unnatural than that which cultivates the inner life, the life of meditation, but neglects the outer life, the life of action.

It is true that there are some apparent exceptions to this statement. Some persons are shut up in close retirement by the afflictions which God sends. Such have to "suffer the will of God," and in so doing come out from themselves and enact their inner spiritual life in their endurance of suffering. Besides this, it is doubtful if there be many instances in which those thus secluded cannot, if they will, "*do* the will of God." A suggestion, a "word in season," a look of submission, a prayer,—how often does the sick saint wield these instrumentalities with power for his master! How often does he by his submission to the divine will show to those about him the beauty of holiness and the glory of God's sustaining grace! The exception mentioned is only apparent.

But in all ordinary cases there must be active obedience to God in all the walks of life. Let me illustrate this thought by referring to a few facts.

PUBLIC WORSHIP.

To develop the Christian manhood to a certain extent, the inner life *must assume some outward religious forms*. A form, however imposing it may be, is as empty as "sounding brass or a tinkling cymbal" if the spirit of religion be not in it. Some reverse this statement, and declare the spirit to be everything and the form nothing. This is an error. If one should say, "I remember Christ and his death every day, and therefore I do not think it obligatory on me to celebrate the Lord's Supper," it might be said to him, "Christ has said, 'This do in remembrance of me,' and you have no right to substitute something else. If you do set aside his command, it is one proof that you have not the spirit of religion, since the rule is, 'If ye love me keep my commandments.' "

Public worship is treated in the Bible as essential to the well-being of society and the growth of piety in the individual Christian. Hence it is that we find this in the old dispensation to be an established principle that people must come together on the Sabbath for worship, praise and instruction. Under the Christian dispensation the same fact is apparent and the same principle enforced: "Let us consider one another to provoke unto love and to good works; *not forsaking the assembling of ourselves together, as the manner of some is,* but exhorting one another; and so much the more as ye see the day approaching."[1]

This is no less an obligation laid by the divine command than it is a necessity growing out of our wants as communities and individuals. Any community which has not public worship will sink in

[1] Heb. x. 24, 25.

morals, and any person who strikes out this grand element of life from his practice will certainly grow indifferent to the claims of religion. Take any Christian professor, however zealous, and let him stay away from public worship any considerable time without a good cause, and it will transform him. Here is the explanation of those sad changes which so often take place in Christians emigrating to new countries. They find no churches, and yield weakly to the difficulties of the case instead of saying: "If we worship in a barn or in the woods, we *must* worship God publicly for our own sake and that of our children."

He who would grow into a sturdy Christian manhood must meet "the great congregation" to worship God if he can. Let him strain his muscles to the utmost from early Monday morning until late Saturday night *in his worldly business*, and then decline to attend church on the Lord's day because he feels tired and worn out, or let him say, "Our singing is not to my liking, our minister's discourses are weak. I have the sermons of the great Master of the pulpit, and I have the Bible, and God is in every place, and I can worship him as well at home as at the church, and much more to my liking." Or let him habitually be deterred from God's house by its being too hot or too cold, too wet or too dry, or by some other excuse which the ingenuity of such persons is quick to suggest, and his piety and his comfort as a Christian will suffer. He may not make his church-going depend on the accidental circumstance that some favorite is to "hold forth the word of life," or absent himself because some one is to preach God's truth who has small gifts wherewith to dazzle or attract. If he be not a habitual attendant on public worship from principle, his piety will wilt as a plant withers when a worm is eating off its root.

Depend upon it, the true Christian who is growing up to a vigorous manhood will long for the courts of the Lord, and feel that they are blessed who dwell in God's house.[1] Said the Psalmist: "One thing have I desired of the Lord, that will I seek after, that I may dwell in the house of the Lord all the days of my life, to behold the beauty of the Lord and to inquire in his temple."[2]

[1] Ps. lxxxiv. 1–4. [2] Ps. xxvii. 4.

FAMILY WORSHIP.

Family worship is another duty which is implied in the organization of the family into the school, the main intention of which is to train the young for heaven.[1] Here we find the means of bringing divine worship each day to bear on the minds of all in the family. It is not enough to go to church on the Sabbath, nor ought parents to content themselves with this. If they do, they and their households will as surely feel the effects of that course as would their bodies if fed only once in seven days. Here the spirit *and* the form of religion are necessary. "What God hath joined together let no man put asunder."

The inner life which communes with God must take form in the outer life, the life of meditation in the soul must take form in this essential relation of life, working itself outwardly for the glory of God in the right training of the family. How true this statement is may be seen in the fact that we can name no vigorous, zealous, heavenly-minded Christian whose inner life does not prompt him to build a family altar on which the fire never goes out. To such a one it is not merely an item

[1] Deut. vi. 3–9.

in the church covenant, irksome, useless and, if possible, to be nullified, but it is a blessed privilege of which the soul avails itself to manifest and promote the glory of God by feeding its own piety and developing the piety of others.

SECRET WORSHIP.

The same is true of *closet devotion.* There must, if possible, be some form through which the inner life expresses itself. The Quaker sits still and waits for the movings of the Spirit, and some Christian professors ask themselves, "What necessity is there for us to enter into our closet and there pray? Why not pray when we are walking or in company or at our business?" This last every Christian ought to do; but let him beware lest he allow this to be an excuse for omitting to comply with Christ's direction: "When thou prayest enter into thy closet, and when thou hast shut thy door pray to thy Father which is in secret."[1] There must be an actual place and a real form of worship. The bowed knee, the closed eye, the articulated prayer for help and in thanksgiving for mercy, must help the worshipper to express his heart-devotions to God in secret.

[1] Matt. vi. 6.

22

Such is the nature God has given us that we must comply with this rule to develop the Christian manhood by allowing the inner life to assume some outward religious forms. There must in all worship be a harmony between the inner life and the outward forms. The professed worshiper who irreverently sits upright, with unclosed eyes, during prayer, public or social, is an uncomely and probably an unprofited object.

CHAPTER XV.

ACTIVE DUTY.

AN OPEN PROFESSION.

SUPPOSE we were to see the body of a man lying on the ground, and that we should hear the physician declare that the man is alive and in vigorous health. We feel for his pulse, but find none; we put our ear to his heart, but can detect no movement; we find his body cold, and cannot perceive that he breathes. He neither walks, nor talks, nor breathes, nor feels, nor acts, and in the face of the most positive assertion to the contrary we would say, "The man is dead, for if he had life in him he would show it in action." But we can believe this child to be alive even when he is motionless in sleep, because his heart beats and his lungs act. When he is awake, the signs of life and health cannot be mistaken. All his senses alive, his glowing cheek and incessant activity cannot be mistaken.

When a sinner is converted he is compared to one who has been raised from the dead.[1] To appreciate this figure recall the scenes which attended the raising of Lazarus to life. As he was laid in the grave, the evidences that he was dead were found in his lack of sensibility to external objects and his inability to do anything. Mary might have knelt at that grave and have poured forth her plaintive grief as she said, "O my brother, come back to us!" and yet that dead body would have shown no signs of feeling. But when Jesus said to him, "Lazarus, come forth," then he arose, he saw, he heard, he felt, he walked, he spake, he ate, he acted. His actions proved him to be alive.

If a sinner has been made alive, he will as certainly show it as Lazarus did his resurrection. This life which shows no action, this alleged conversion which shows no change, this good tree which brings not forth good fruit, is an impossibility. We use salt, and it will season and preserve flesh; we light a candle, and it will shine; we put life into a heart, and it will beat; and so

[1] Eph. ii. 1; Col. ii. 13.

also, when God breathes into man's nostrils the breath of life, he will become a living soul, showing his life by doing what God commands him to do.

But what must a Christian man *do* in order that he may not merely and barely demonstrate that he is alive, but that he may be a vigorous man? One thing he must do—he must *openly profess his faith in Christ.* Some think that religion is a matter solely between each man and God in such a sense that a man can keep his religion secret like a concealed charm. This does not tally with the Scriptures. Thus, when Moses found Israel worshiping the golden calf, he stood in the gate of the camp, and said, "Who is on the Lord's side? let him come unto me." Elijah said to the people on Mount Carmel, "How long halt ye between two opinions? If the Lord be God, follow him; but if Baal, then follow him." Our blessed Lord said, "He that is not with me is against me: and he that gathereth not with me scattereth abroad." "For whosoever shall be ashamed of me and of my words, of him shall the Son of man be ashamed when he shall come in his own glory, and in his Father's and of the holy angels." "Wherefore come out from among them, and be ye separate, saith the Lord."[1]

Where two parties are opposed to each other, even when there is enough of human fallibility to prove that neither may be entirely right, concealed friendship is regarded with no little displeasure. But when one party is entirely right and the other wrong, any attempt to walk so near the dividing line as to render it doubtful to which party a man belongs is regarded with no favor. God has a controversy with a world of rebels, and he commands every loyal subject to let that loyalty appear so clearly that no one will be in doubt whether he is on the devil's side or on God's. What was thought during our Revolution of the men who pretended to love their country, and yet aided her enemies with intelligence, food and shelter? or of those who stood no one knew where?

If a man have religion in his heart, it will incline him to number himself as one of God's people. It may not be charitable to say that a real Christian may not be kept back from a public profession, but that it will be in the face of God's directions and to his most serious injury,

[1] 2 Cor. vi. 17.

we do assert. Who can name a bright, lively, active, joyful Christian who has not performed this duty?

ACTIVE DUTY—WORKS OF FAITH.

It is evident that a mere profession of faith in Christ is not enough. If a merchant should advertise for a bookkeeper, and a young man should profess to be the possessor of that knowledge, the question determining his qualifications would be not what he *professes* to do, but what he actually *does*. He would not be continued a week on any profession of his own or recommendation of others unless these were shown to be deserved by his work.

It is a notorious fact that a physician who should make loud profession of ability and skill would be frowned on as a quack if in the treatment of patients he should show no skill.

It is so in the duties which grow out of the various relations which men hold to God and one another. Professions in order to command confidence must be accompanied by works. The profession of piety is no exception to the general rule.

If, then, a sinner *professes* to have in his soul

the inner life of piety, what in addition to a profession must he *do* in the way of *works* in order to the development of a strong Christian manhood?

A Consistent Life.

The very nature of that inward change which he professes to have experienced shows that *he must glorify God by a consistent life among men.* This direction is one that is more easily understood than defined. A certain Christian professor once called on a sick woman to pray with and comfort her in her trouble. After he had spoken a few words of sympathy and prayed with her he left the room. As the door closed she said to an unconverted daughter: "There goes a good man!" Some years ago a Christian man, the governor of one of our States, learned that a stranger was very sick at a public-house, and forthwith, as a Christian and church officer, he visited the sick man, spoke to him about Jesus, and then prayed with him. Said the person who stated the fact: "I there saw what is not often seen—the governor of a State as a Christian elder visiting and praying with the stranger who was sick." And who that hears the fact does not say at once: "This certainly is a good man. Here is a Christian who lives a consistent life among men!"

There is a way of living—a demeanor—which commands the approbation of people who are very apt to say of him who thus lives: "He is a good man," and of another who does not thus live: "He is not a Christian—at least, he does not act like one."

Many years ago in a populous town a Christian professor was conducting a large and popular school. A new pupil was entered, and a few days afterward surprised the relative with whom he was boarding by asking whether Mr. —— was a member of the church. He was answered in the affirmative, and then the inquiry was made of him: "Why do you ask such a question? Does not Mr. —— live like a Christian?"

"I should think not," was the boy's answer, "for I have been there a week, and he has not opened the school with prayer once, nor read the Scriptures to us, nor said one word which would show that he cared anything about our souls. When he punishes the boys he does it cruelly, and I have not seen anything in his conduct which looked as if he were a Christian."

His reasoning was just. This man was occupying a place of great importance, and he was bound to live a Christian life *there among those pupils.* If the inner life of piety had been vigorous, it would have shaped his outer life in such a glorious sphere for doing good.

A young Christian went from home into new associations, and one of his acquaintances was asked concerning his course. The reply was: "He lives very consistently. His employer speaks in glowing terms of his conduct, and in our church he is a very active Christian."

It must be thus in every position which the Christian fills. In the family, the shop, the store, the field, the office, the school, the social gathering, the religious meeting—whatever the position in order to be a perfect man who has come to the measure of the stature of Christ, he must glorify God by a consistent life. He must let his light shine before men.

WINNING SOULS.

He must also work to win souls to Christ. In other words, he must strive to extend the dominion of Christ among mankind.

This world is given to Christ as the reward for his suffering the penalty of the Law in the place of sinners.[1] The subjugation of this world to Christ is to be effected through human instrumentality. Using a military figure, the apostle calls Jesus the captain of our salvation. His soldiers are converted sinners, and to them he says, "Go ye into all the world and preach the gospel to every creature." By a happy phrase these converted sinners, banded together in one army for the conquest of the world, are called "the Church militant." Jesus, the captain of this host, has appointed certain officers whose main business is to organize and train the rank and file of the Church for the most efficient action, and to lead them in the conflict. All the members of this army, both officers and soldiers, have a work to do, and in order to the highest efficiency each one must do his own work with promptness and energy.

And how do military commanders secure manliness and efficiency in their troops? *By actual service.* As a sentinel the soldier must watch, he must keep himself trained for service, when ordered to march he must march, and when ordered to charge or resist the enemy he must obey. It is not by sleeping when he ought to be awake, or by resting when he ought to be active, that he be-

[1] Ps. ii. 8; Isa. liii. 2.

comes a manly and valiant soldier. Hence says the apostle to Timothy: "Fight the good fight of faith," and in another connection he tells him the secret of his own rugged Christian manhood: "I have fought a good fight, I have finished my course, I have kept the faith."[1] Active exertion as the necessary condition of a vigorous manhood is set forth by this great soldier in various ways. "This one thing I do: forgetting those things which are behind and reaching forth unto those things which are before, I press toward the mark for the prize of the high calling of God in Christ Jesus."[2] Very impressively does he teach the same truth in telling his fellow-soldiers to put on the whole armor of God that they may be able to withstand in the evil day.[3]

But one main thing which the Christian soldier is to do is to rescue sinners from the dominion of Satan. When he himself fled from the camp of Satan, renouncing all allegiance to "the god of this world," he did not come to the camp of Christ merely to hide himself behind the ramparts and find some safe and pleasant retreat whence he is never to go to fight the enemy. He

[1] 1 Tim. vi. 12; 2 Tim. iv. 7. [2] Phil. iii. 13, 14.
[3] Eph., vi. 10–18.

is to do what he can to rescue those who are in the dreadful captivity from which by the grace of God he has escaped.

To drop the figure, as soon as a sinner is converted he is to seek the conversion of others. If he be a parent, he must strive to win his children to Christ; if he be a teacher, he must try to lead his scholars to Christ; if he be a mechanic or merchant or farmer or lawyer or physician, he must not forget that he is to wield his influence with the wisdom of the serpent and the harmlessness of the dove to win those about him to Christ. He is not to be a mere earth-bowed servant of the muck-rake, with painful toil collecting treasures that moth and rust can corrupt and thieves can steal. No, he is to work with energy to lead souls to Christ. If he do not, he is recreant to duty, and he will damage his own Christian manhood. There never was a vigorous manhood produced in any age or circumstances when the real convert did not put forth direct, positive and earnest effort to lead sinners to God, to turn many to righteousness. If any Christian professor neglects this duty, let him not wonder that his faith is weak, his hope dim, his comforts small, his graces dead, his efficiency as near nothing as possible. Let him work for Christ, and Christ will make his strength perfect in weakness.

Here is the vital difficulty with the attempt to be a Christian *secretly*. If a man be alive, he will show it to others by his actions, but to have the Christian life in one's soul, and yet not show that life by breath, by look, by word, by effort, this seems *incredible*, not to say *impossible*.

SELF-DENIAL.

The Christian soldier *must deny himself for Christ*. He is not to live a life of ease and self-indulgence. He must take up his CROSS and follow Christ. He cannot "strive to enter in at the strait gate" without denying ungodliness and worldly lusts.[1] He must abstain from all appearance of evil,[2] and also from acts which in themselves may be innocent, for the good of those who are weak.[3] Many restraints on his own inclinations he must lay, and many sacrifices for the good of others he must make. Jesus, his Master and Saviour, is carrying on a costly war against principalities and powers, against the rulers of the

[1] Luke xiii. 24; Tit. ii. 12. [2] 1 Thess. v. 22.
[3] Rom. xiv. 13-23; 1 Cor. viii. 9; x. 23.

darkness of this world, and spiritual wickedness in high places, and he commands his redeemed ones to help him with their property. He cannot be guiltless if at such a time he has never denied himself some innocent gratification to help forward the cause of Him who, though he was rich, for our sakes became poor. Much to be pitied and to be blamed art thou, O Christian who hast never denied thy appetite, thy love of ease or personal adornment in order to have something to aid forward the cause of Christ.

Self-denial for the sake of Christ and a fallen world is one of the necessary parts of that training which develops and glorifies the Christian manhood, and it were as easy to train a Greek athlete without right food and exercise as to train a perfect Christian man without self-denial.

PROMOTING THE GOOD OF SOCIETY.

He must exercise himself in every work which promotes the good of society. Said the apostle, "Put them in mind . . . . to be ready to every good work."[1] Christian people are "to walk worthy of the Lord unto all pleasing, being fruitful in every good work."[2] The Christian is a

[1] Tit. iii. 1.

[2] Col. i. 10.

citizen, and as such he must pray and work for the good of his country. He may not be a bad citizen, corrupting the morals of citizens, resisting the laws of the land and elevating bad men to places of power. He is a member of society, and he must be truthful, honest, benevolent, public-spirited, in order that society may become more virtuous as the years pass away. In blessing the world with those institutions which educate the young for usefulness, relieve the distresses of the unfortunate and restore the fallen, the Christian may not be like a snail living in its own narrow shell. His influence must be felt in organizing the common school and giving it a Christian character; in founding and invigorating the Christian college, the Christian almshouse, the Christian hospital, the Christian asylum. A Christian man cannot attain a vigorous manhood if he shut himself up in his own little house, never planting a tree, or moving a stone, or opening a fountain, or beautifying a path, or adding force to a school, or imparting good influence to social customs and institutions.

THREE IMPORTANT DIRECTIONS.

The development of character admits of a vast variety. One is a strong Christian, another a weak one; one is a joyful Christian, another a desponding one; one is as onward in his course "as the shining light which shineth more and more unto the perfect day," another is "unstable in all his ways," and is very liable to be "turned aside after Satan;" one Christian, like an arch, is made stronger and firmer by the very loads which to the undiscerning eye seem tending to destroy him, another is like a reed easily broken. Two Christians may leave the same church and community to find a home among strangers who are not favorable to practical piety. The one will quietly yet resolutely assert his office as a candle which is to shine in the midst of darkness, whilst the other will allow himself to be extinguished. Follow the one where you will, and you find that he has moulded others to his views, and won for religion a position in the regards of those about him. Follow the other one where you will, and you find no Bethels or Ebenezers which he has erected in the midst of a gainsaying world. One Christian professor may live so as to excite no suspicion as to his profession among strangers, whilst another lives so as to be an epistle of Christ known and read of all men. A pastor dismisses one Christian with no fear as to his demeanor in other connections, but he stands in doubt of another, fearing that he has bestowed his labor on him in vain.

There is probably not a community in which there are not some who have professed Christ, but when transplanted to other circumstances whose piety has withered away. The apostle wrote in his Epistle to the Romans: "Salute my well beloved Epenetus, who is the first fruits of Achaia unto Christ."[1] This man, converted in Greece, removed to Rome, the capital of the world, and yet had not lost his religion by the removal. But many a man who believed that he was a Christian at the North has not carried his religion to the South, and many a professed convert at the East has found the Alleghanies or the Mississippi an impassable barrier to his piety. This lamentable fact attends the emigration of people from old to new countries, and also from the country to the town, or from the town to the country.

[1] Rom. xvi. 5.

In our country and times communities are liable to great changes. The West invites the emigrant with the promise that present discomforts shall be made up with large gains in the end. The city holds up its powerful inducements to the enterprising to go thither in the expectation of being one of the fortunate ones who shall seize the golden prize. The mechanical occupations and the learned professions are constantly inviting (especially the young) to change. Within twelve years from a single country parish at least a hundred young people have been scattered abroad, some to the West, some to the South, some to the slopes of the Pacific, some to the city, some here and some there. Every year changes are going on, and it becomes a question of great moment, "How can these young people be guarded from harm in these frequent changes?" If a young man were to ask for a word of counsel as he is about to go from home, among other things the following might be given:

KEEPING THE SABBATH.

The young person who would secure stability of religious character must keep the Sabbath holy, let the hindrances be never so great. Those who have narrowly observed the influence of this direction on young people going from home are unanimous here. In our academies and colleges there are peculiar temptations, not openly to profane the Sabbath, but to accommodate and lessen the requirements of that day to a standard which allows the reading of books, the attention to studies and to social intercourse which do as really violate the commandment as pleasure excursions on land or water. The student is not under the inspection of his parents, and is tempted to regard his attendance on public worship once or twice on the Sabbath as a fulfillment of the fourth commandment.

It is a fact that many a Christian professor has gone back from his high position after entering an educational institution. The gold becomes dim and the fine gold is changed. Many a young man has gone thither with the design of entering the ministry, and yet some insidious influence has wrought a change, until he has barely maintained his place in the church or has become "a castaway." So fearfully frequent at one time were these defections as almost to paralyze all efforts to educate young men for the ministry. And one cause for so sad a change first showed itself in their either openly or virtually repudiating the Sabbath as a day to be devoted to religious purposes. Perhaps the young man, ambitious to excel in his class, secretly uses a few hours of the Sabbath in study, or he is interested in general literature, and finding that his hours of leisure during the week for that object are few, he takes a portion of the Sabbath to read Gibbon or Hume or Prescott or Bancroft. It will not take long for him to be hardened enough to read on that day Scott or Cooper, Dickens or Byron or Shelley. We have seen an apple which seemed very fair and sound, but beneath the skin it was rotten to the very core. Thus has many a student's religion sunk to a mere exterior under the corrupting force of Sabbath-breaking.

The temptation to this dangerous course is extreme with the young who go from home to engage in some laborious occupation. The six days of labor are used up, and when the Lord's day comes the mechanic or laborer is tempted to spend it in bed, in lounging or improper reading, or conversation, or some sort of pleasure-seeking. The excuse is that he is tired and that the Sabbath is a day of rest. A youth whose piety apparently was quite above the ordinary level went to the city to learn a trade. After a time his religious zeal suffered a decline, and, whilst he did not give up his hope in Christ, he did not have that life and joy he once had. A casualty laid him on his deathbed, and he told his mother with tears the secret of his religious declension. Following a very tiresome occupation, he had been misled by some companions to think that he could best spend the Sabbath by walking abroad among the works of nature. Did he not need rest, and could he not get it more readily in this way than by attending church and strictly observing the Sabbath? What the consequences would have been had not God interposed no one can tell, but one thing is evident—his mistake in this respect did him a great injury, and shaded with regrets the close of his life, although no one doubted his piety.

A little more than forty years ago several families removed from New Jersey to Ohio. In the wilderness there was no church, and they had not force enough to maintain the Sabbath as a day of religious observance. It took only a year or two to reduce them to such a situation that they hardly hoped they were Christians, and they cared but little about the matter.

The Sabbath is a corner-stone in the temple of Christian experience. Tear that out, and the building will sooner or later fall. We have a striking illustration of this in the Germans, who under the mistaken lead of Luther have degraded the Sabbath from its high and sacred position. They, to a very great extent, seem plunging into hopeless infidelity, and in this country the Christian Sabbath has no fiercer opponents than they. But as one after another is converted he restores the Sabbath to its proper place.

In other words, if either a community or a person neglect or trample on the Sabbath which God commands all to keep holy, the transgressor will show the effects of that sin in a deteriorated character and a degenerating piety. Hence it is that we so often warn young Christians, when about to leave home, that their future Christian course will very much depend on the manner in which they keep the Sabbath.

IDENTIFICATION WITH CHRISTIANS.

If a young Christian would secure stability of character, let him *be careful to identify himself with God's cause and people.* There is scarcely anything more unfortunate for a young Christian than to be entangled in the net of a false position. Doubtless many a one might trace his religious declension back to this source. It is a humiliating and very difficult confession to make that we were weak enough when joining some new community to act a part which seemed to say, "We are not Christians. Nay, we are the world's people! We are not so weak as to be religious and associate with religious people!" When once that position is taken, a person cannot content himself with merely being there, but he must do something to show himself worthy of being there. He will overcome his scruples so as to walk or ride for pleasure on the Sabbath, or read some book, or engage in some occupation unbecoming the Sabbath. One wrong step leads to another until he is entangled so greatly as to baffle his efforts to extricate himself.

To illustrate this, the case of a young man may be cited who went to a new country in quest of business. He had made a profession of religion, but took no certificate with him. He found a very different state of things from that which he had left. Profaneness, Sabbath-breaking, intemperance, every style of dancing and carousing, gambling, horse-racing, and such like vices, were common. Many men of high social position indulged in these sinful ways as a matter of course. Religious people were in the minority, and their observances were regarded with contempt or treated with hostility. To be a religious man in that region required decision, and while his conscience approved the religious course, his courage was not equal to the task of practicing it. No one knew him there, and the concealment of his opinions and former professions was not difficult. He did not by act or word say to his new acquaintances, "I am a Christian man by profession, and am resolved to be one in practice." If he went to church on a communion-day, he never seated himself with the communicants; he never attended the prayer-meeting, and no one suspected that he ever prayed. He was recognized and treated as one of the world. No one thought it out of place to invite him to a dancing-party or ball, or to some gay festivity on the Sabbath. Having weakly chosen to conceal his profession, he was treated by the world as one of its own members, and he was obliged to act accordingly.

By and by what was at first difficult became easy, and he dropped into the world's ranks as if he had never taken the vows of God upon him.

He committed a fatal mistake when he did not quietly but *openly* take his position on the Lord's side and with his people. That step would have won him the battle by bringing him God's favor, by giving him strength and by forestalling the temptations of his position. It is said that Mr. Calhoun of South Carolina was never challenged to fight a duel, because he boldly took the position that that mode of settling differences was unreasonable and wrong. And thus the young Christian who removes to the city or to the West will find a manly avowal of his profession at the very outset will be a shield to him from very many temptations.

The importance of this advice cannot be overestimated, and it is illustrated by numberless sad examples as well as by not a few bright ones. Apprentices, young mechanics, students, professional men, merchants, men leaving the country for the city, or the East for the West, have given proof that it is a mighty safeguard to a Christian entering into society among strangers to identify himself at once with God's cause and people, and that to do otherwise is an expedient no more dangerous than wicked. Let no Christian among strangers sail under doubtful colors, but let him by his life and words hoist a bannei on which the world may see this inscription, "I AM THE LORD'S."

A CHURCH HOME.

The Christian who would secure stability and vigor of character *must have a home in some one Christian church.* The superiority of one church over another, as if one's success as a Christian depended on his attendance there, is not here advocated. There is a great temptation to allow personal caprice or some trivial and unessential circumstance to supplant principles in the matter of attending church services. If a man has been educated in a particular form of religious faith, he ought not to abandon that faith without a good reason. If a man has been trained a Roman Catholic or a Presbyterian, let him not renounce his faith without an appeal to God's word, and planting himself on the eternal principles of right. To become a Baptist merely to gratify a friend, or a Methodist because of the preaching of a gifted minister, or a Presbyterian because some obnoxious minister or member may be in the church which the man usually attends, is to degrade the Christian profession. When one takes a step so important, he ought to be able to "give a reason for the hope that is in him." It is undoubtedly a fact most lamentable that thousands decide the question, "What communion shall we join?" by determining the bearings of the step on their social popularity, their success in business, or some other equally sordid motive. The results are very painful and often disgraceful, indicating that a lack of Christian principle in determining what church they would join was a proof that the love of God was not in them.

In the frequent changes which are taking place among churches, we find a danger which besets migrating Christians, whether going to some new country or to some town or city. The danger is that the emigrant may lose his *home* in the church, and this danger is increased by the difficulties of finding such a home, or the temptation to go now to this church and now to the other, wandering from one place to another until the *home feeling is all gone.* When that is gone, one of the most effective incentives to duty and restraints from wrong has been taken away. The Christian who would have vigor and effectiveness must have a church home, a place in which he expects to worship the Lord, a locality around which centre the powerful associations of

Christian fellowship and life. You may examine this matter extensively, and you will find that your ripe, vigorous, growing Christians have their home in some one church, and that when they leave that it is as when a man of right tastes and affections leaves his own home for a time; he leaves it with regret, he returns to it with gladness.

Let a young man remove to either of the neighboring cities, and allow himself to depart from this idea, that he *must have a home in some one church;* let him on Sabbath morning go to one church because they have a brilliant preacher, in the afternoon to another because the building is so beautiful, and in the evening to another because the music is so good; the next Sabbath let him attend the cathedral in the morning, the Swedenborgian in the afternoon and the Universalist in the evening; let him attend now the Presbyterian, now the Methodist and now the Baptist, now the Episcopal and now the Papal, and in a little time as a Christian he will be demoralized. He has no home, no Christian fellowship, no special duties growing out of these, no higher incentive to the Christian life than the curiosity to hear some preacher, to see some elegant church edifice or be present at some novel religious ceremony.

What is the result? His taste for novelty becomes satiated, his principles are damaged, and in all probability he will lose his interest not merely in one church, but in all churches, and make shipwreck of his Christian character. The cases are not few in which this has been the highway which vacillating Christians have followed until it has led them back into the world more hardened than when they began a religious life. The Christian professor who, when removing from one place to another, does not find for himself a home in some one church, will not merely find his piety and his religious principles deteriorating and his virtues dimmed, but that such a course persisted in will be proof that he was self-deceived or a hypocrite.

We cannot be too emphatic or urgent here in calling upon Christian emigrants, as soon as Providence will let them, to find a home in some one church.

CHAPTER XVI.

THE CONCLUSION OF THE WHOLE MATTER.

IN bringing these discussions to a close, it would savor of egotism in the writer to express the honesty of his own purpose to benefit all his Christian brethren, and especially the younger portion of them, by discussing some great principles and truths which have an important bearing on their well-being in this life and that beyond death. Whilst not slow to acknowledge how much self-condemnation these discussions and illustrations have wrought in himself, nor the unceasing anxiety he has felt that his brethren should be aided to assume a higher position and to assert the life of Christ in the heart with more power, he brings no railing accusation in saying it is his confident belief that many live so far beneath their privileges as to have comparatively little confidence in their own religion and very little of that joyous and soaring faith which, even as a bird sings in the morning, chants ir the darkest day and under the very portals of death: "I know whom I have believed." When the heart is full of love to God, who first loved us, to Christ, who died for us, and to our fellow-men, for whom Christ died as he did for us, when the will and purpose of our heart to serve Christ drive us to acts and works and self-denials, when our lives and our hearts, our actions and our feelings, are in harmony, concentrating on the one object of glorifying God by saving men,—then God will allow us to walk in the high places of the earth, he will lift up our heads above our enemies round about, will allow us to turn many unto righteousness, and whilst giving us these signs of his love, he will also permit us to rejoice with exceeding joy, so that life shall be made up of successful labor and consequent joy, and the terrors of death be overcome by the ministrations of those angel visitants who convoy the souls of God's faithful servants from earth to heaven.

But to his young Christian brethren the writer of these pages would address himself as a father to his beloved children, with yearnings for their welfare and happiness. To you life is yet young, the field of labor is only just entered. Some of you may not remain here long to bear the heat and burden of the day, others will be spared to toil and bear the responsibilities of the Church. To all he would say with earnestness and tender concern, *The secret of success and happiness in the Christian life is found in being full of love of Christ and in giving that love expression in the daily duties of life.* Oh, *be* thus and *live* thus, and you shall gather your precious sheaves for Christ. As you draw near to death you can say: "Yea, though I walk through the valley of the shadow of death, I will fear no evil, for thou art with me, thy rod and thy staff they comfort me." And as you come to the judgment-seat you shall hear Jesus saying to you: "Well done, good and faithful servants, enter ye into the joy of your Lord!"

THE END.

www.ingramcontent.com/pod-product-compliance
Lightning Source LLC
LaVergne TN
LVHW010217110826
845151LV00004B/1121

* 9 7 8 1 4 2 5 5 2 7 5 0 1 *